PLACE OF THE HEART

Life on Fat Hummingbird Farm

Linda H.Y. Hegland

Other Works: Bird Slips, Moon Glows

(a book of poetry) 2019

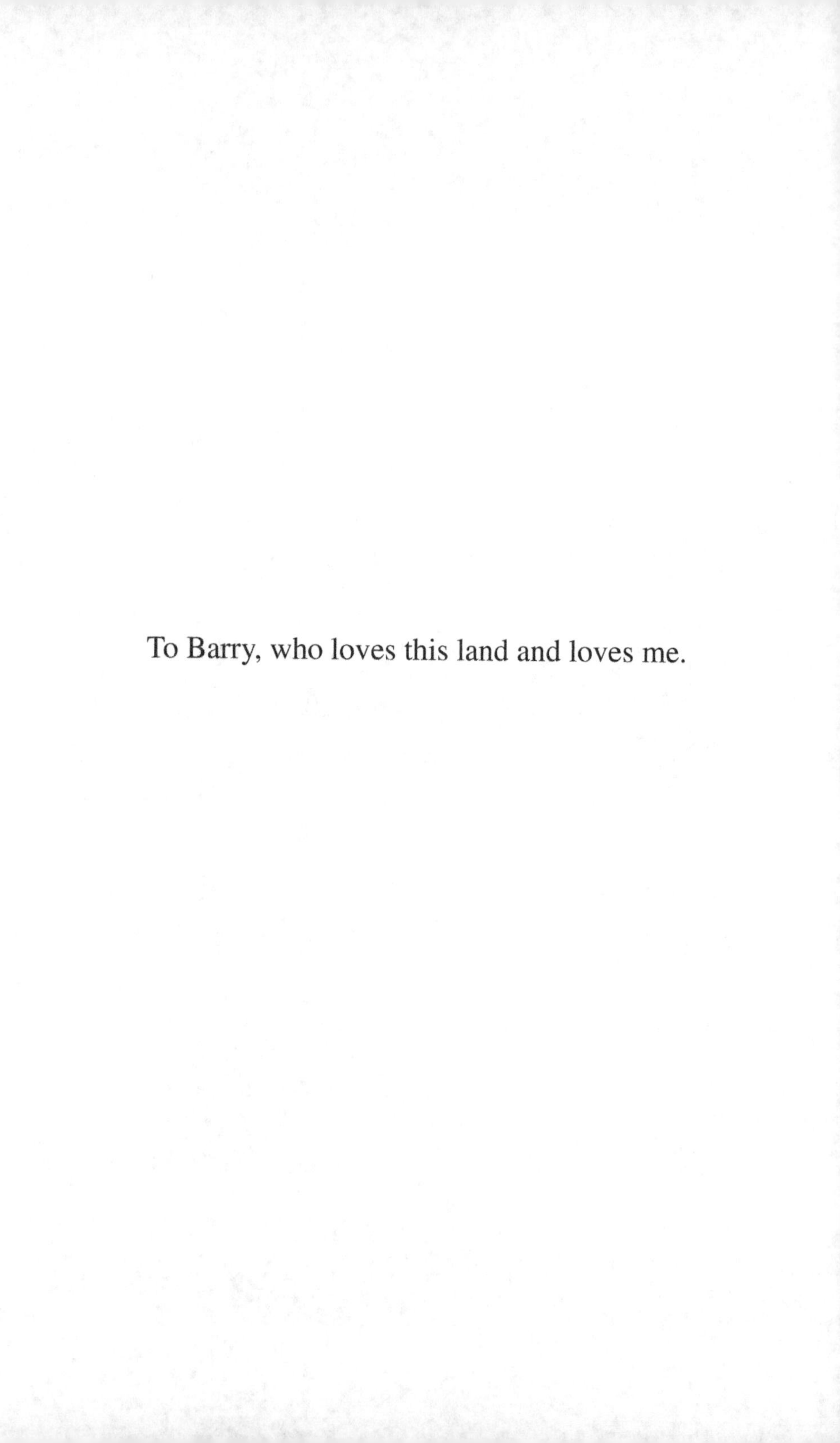

To Barry, who loves this land and loves me.

PREFACE

I have moved to where my heart longed to be. I have drifted in my life, now to the foot of a mountain; with acres of grass and meadow and woods and ancient orchards that hide beneath the soil; and cows that low in the morning fog and butterflies that dance above the goldenrod.

My dreamed longings have married with the view.

It is quiet. I no longer hear the backdrop of the swish and whirr of continual traffic or colliding trains in the machine-deafening train yard; the overheard angry conversations and the frightening siren sounds late at night.

It is loud. It is cacophonous with the sounds of horses, and cows, and chickens, and dogs, and crickets, and frogs, and cicadas; the whooping shrieks of the coywolves chasing the arcing moon, the calls and twitters and whistles and songs of so many, many birds my head whirls with trying to know them.

And the wind – that comes up from the bay and over the mountain to dance with our trees in the woods. And has many songs – but never sings with the fog.

This place, this humble farm and its more than three centuries of history; this place of verdant woods and gentle meadow and (occasionally) salt-tanged air, this place we have named Fat Hummingbird Farm, is an artist. She spins the gossamer clouds into mare's tails. She paints the meadows with wildflowers and butterflies. She forms gullies and streams with the soil and water and pulls lichen-scabbed stones from the earth. She sings – always.

I am now her noviciate. I am here, at the foot of the mountain, and my heart is receptive, welcoming – to put into photographs what is shown me, and to put into poetic line what is taught me. Like the silent, eye-filled woods at night, or the shimmer of the sleeping river, or the hush of the listening moon. In this place where, unbeknownst to me all these years, I am meant to be.

Contents

THE PRESENCE IN WOOD SCREEN DOORS

Our farmhouse is old - 150 years, in fact. It has places where doors used to be and places where you imagine doors should be. Sometimes noon shadows on the floor meet at the wall at an angle that suggest a door - a door made of dust motes and sun. As the house settles over the years, bricks part ways - doors open in cracks, slam in crevices. At night, doors are suggested in the light of the moon; a blacker black against the dark of the night. The opening and shutting doors of a house can sometimes just be seen in the corner of your eye. If you stare too long, they disappear.

Our house has three wooden screen doors. They remind me so much of the doors of the old farmhouse in which I spent a lot of my summers growing up - the home of the grandparents of a family friend. Numerous children all the day long slammed in and out, in and out, of those screen doors; followed by the fruitless admonition - "Don't slam the screen door . . . !" There is such a snugness in the creaking sound of the wood and metal as it rasps back and forth on its hinges. In the humid hot weather, or again in the icy cold, the doors swell and stick - become stubborn. In my childhood, June bugs hung on the screens. As we sat in the dimly-lit living room, a radio tuned to the stories read on the CBC, we could hear the constant tick, tick, tick as their armoured bodies landed on the screens. Later, we would hear the scratching and scuttling of the nails of the barn cats as they came to feed on the June bugs. Here, on Fat Hummingbird Farm, lacy smears of gold-coloured spider's eggs cling instead. Moths spread their wings like mottled lace against the weave of the screen. At night, the sound of crickets seeps through the screen mesh. And each of those screen doors closes with an inevitable slam.

ABANDONED BARNS

I love old falling-down barns! I love their sadness and their clinging resilience as weeds and weather and time inescapably pull them to the ground. Inside a barn there is a whole world in and of itself. Stepping into one is like crossing a threshold. Hay turned to dust that cakes the inside of your nostrils and coats the floor. The light shining through the cracks in the wall and roof creating tiger stripes of sun and shadow wallpaper. Old rope hangs from the rafters, binding twine festoons the beams, an old moldering saddle in the dusty corner of a stall is home to a family of wee mice. Rusting pocketknives atop rotted hay bales and tangled fishing line at the end of a dry and split fishing rod tell stories of young boys that played here long, long ago. Escaping to the pond after a hot morning of chores.

We don't have any abandoned barns on Fat Hummingbird Farm. But on properties all up and down the mountain and along our country road there are plenty. There is one on a little used road up the mountain. It stands - well slumps - in a field that seems to hold little else but the barn and wildflowers and a stone-bubbled track that appears to have been recently used by a truck. A barn growing its own world. I can imagine abandoned barns when they were painted red and housed sweet-smelling hay and the piquant sweat of horses. When the sun-sparked dust motes floated above cows laying in straw and manure chewing their cuds methodically. As a child on the friend's grandparents' farm we would play on the second floor of the barn and amongst its hundreds of stacked hay bales. There was nothing up there but hay, sunshine, dust, hidden litters of kittens, pigeons, and the secret games of children rosy with sun-roasted cheeks and the blooming lust of our first puerile kisses. We would slide hollering down the hay chute into the feed troughs of feeding cows and laugh at their astonished and confounded faces as we appeared beneath their noses.

Old barns crumble in overgrown fields, slump in the corner of meadows, cling to the side of a road. I cannot seem to pass them by. Some people love old churches. I love old barns more than churches. Even in their dying, they sing the sunshine that pours through their rotting rafters. I can love that song.

THE HEART OF A HOUSE

Old houses, even abandoned houses, are not empty. They are filled with memories. They are filled with voices. Arguments, laughter, song, the sweet words of love uttered at the end of the day in a shared bed. Old houses breathe. They have a heart beat.

There is an old, abandoned house up near the end of our road. Nature is reclaiming it bit by bit, the ivy seeping into every crack and cranny and clinging tightly there. Its roof shingles curl, the paint rains flakes. The windows stare with seemingly no life behind them. It is an incredibly sad, but also an incredibly brave house. All abandoned houses are that - brave. I do know that it was built about the same time as our house - about 150 years ago. Imagine the history, the families, the stories. I've always wished houses could speak - surely no louder than husky whispers, but don't all things yearn to tell us their stories?

I noticed a ladder that lay along the slant of the roof, up to the highest bedroom window in the peak of the roof. When I was 13 or 14, I was seeing a boy that had such a ladder on his roof. On the dark, moonlit evenings we would climb out of his bedroom window and down the ladder to the spot on the sagging roof that our butts just fitted nicely into. Below us, through the window open to the night breeze, we could hear his parents watching the Ed Sullivan show or perhaps playing a rather competitive game of Parcheesi. His father was an especially sore loser. "Oh now, John", we would hear his mother say, "Now watch your temper, it's just a game".

We would sit, clinging to that ladder, and he would enjoy an illicit cigarette and I would enjoy just staring at him (I was, after all, only 13 and quite prone to adoration). I look at the ladder now on this abandoned house and wonder who sat there over the decades and decades. And who adored who.

THE RURAL MAILBOX

At the end of our lane, across the road, is our rural mailbox. It sits atop a post at the side of our meadow - which once was an orchard. It does not yet have a sign attached indicating that the mail is being delivered to Fat Hummingbird Farm - but it will. The mail is delivered by a wee white car with a flashing yellow light on top. When we have mail, the red flag on the box is put up. This mail 'event' has become a very important part of the day. We have a pair of binoculars on the kitchen windowsill - the window that faces the road. Several times throughout the morning I peer through the binoculars to see if the red flag is standing at attention. A thrill runs through me when I see that the diminutive car (usually unseen) has been by and the red flag beckons to me to come and see what surprises may be waiting. The walk down the lane to pick up the mail is bristling with anticipation. It has been a long time since I have felt this way about the mail.

I've always felt there is something sanctified, even sacred, about pieces of paper with scraps of thoughts, ideas, opinions, love, or connection travelling about the earth from place to place, hand to hand, heart to heart. Years and years ago, over 30 years now, some mail I received was very special. I have an artist friend, a good friend then and a good friend now - though we have seen each other perhaps only half a dozen times over those 30 years. A friendship that has endured for a very long time. But there came a time, those 30 years ago, when my husband and myself and our two boys moved far away, to a different life. But the artist wrote letters.

The letters came every few weeks and were fat and bulky, taped together with wads of tape. The letter itself was always at least 10 pages long, hand-written. Newspaper and magazine articles, art cards, gallery opening announcements, snippets of information about the place we had left behind were included. Sometimes photos of her children. Each letter was a little gift of time, thought, and effort. An aspect that was especially enjoyed by our postman were the drawings all over the outside of the envelope. They almost obscured the address and were scrawled over the stamps - something I'm sure the post office did not sanction.

She drew tiny ink pictures of horses grazing with deer. Or horses lying curled on the ground or with noses turned up to a bulbous moon. She drew pictures of her dog, Togo, a dog one of my sons particularly adored. She drew pictures of a pony she had that had victoriously bucked off each of my sons, appropriately named Bucky. A kind of rite of passage, I suppose, being on one's butt in the dust while a pint-sized pony trots smugly off into a prairie sunset.

The letters the artist wrote, and the letters I wrote in return, were a still but forceful song of friendship; a song of the shared thoughts and communal confidences that bound us together as individuals, mothers, and artists. Within those pages, each to the other, were the intertwined words made up of stories of family, motherhood, aging, and creativity.

I kept those letters, with everything that was gorged into them, with the envelopes festooned with drawings, for a very very long time. They travelled with us from house to house, from place to place. The pages grew yellowed and the edges of the envelopes became soft, felted, and torn. Until one day I just didn't have them anymore. Perhaps they got lost when moving, or moldered in a damp basement, or just like so much of the ephemera of our lived lives they were simply no more.

That rural mailbox at our farm, with the red flag that hints at possible surprises? I think each time I open the flap, I hope to find letters. Especially ones with envelopes where horses gallop with deer across our address . . . and Togo howls at the stamp.

THE ART OF PORCH

One of the things that drew us to this house was its front porch. I remember front porches from my childhood. How people sat at night, rocking and talking. Or just sitting and thinking. Sometimes they had a glass of whiskey or a beer at hand. Usually we children sat at their feet and played card games - Go Fish or War. The front porches went away. You rarely see them anymore - in the cities, in the suburbs. But this house is old. It remembers the art that is 'porch'.

It's September, a time of cool freshened mornings when the fog settles on the pastures and meadows like smoke before sunrise. Morning coffee on the front porch is now less a process of escaping the summer heat of the house and more about noting the last of the hummingbird visits and watching summer mellow before our eyes. Afternoon beer or cider on the front porch is about conversations with people who see us on the porch and come up to visit and chat, or perhaps just wave.

Our front porch is our sanctuary, we spend a lot of time there. It wraps around the entire front of the house. It has strewn about it, several old antique chairs - three of them rocking chairs. The various colours of sunlight - yellow, gold, red or white - stream in aslant so that everything is lit in a way that is true and luminous. Two thirds of the porch is covered, so as to enable us to sit out there protected in the rain or from the steady push of the afternoon winds. The porch at the very front of the house is not covered - splendid for staring up at the cimmerian night sky with its millions of stars and solitary changing moon, accompanied by the chorus of crickets and peepers.

The porch is much more than an entryway to our home. Instead it is a place of welcome, celebration, conversation, . . . musing. Here we met the brother of a neighbour, visiting from across the country. We sat and chatted and ate cheese and crackers and talked about when he was a secondary teacher. He left us as a new friend. Here we have hosted friends invited for wine and conversation. We never did make it inside, even as the evening closed in. Here friends and we have gravitated after a shared dinner, to share further dessert and wine. Here we have learned from people the history of our house and of our land. Here we have had long conversations with a FedEx driver about his family and his pride in his high school graduating daughter, and the things he sees on his long days of delivering all over the county.

From this porch, we have watched summer thunder storms and local parades of cyclists as they dart by in an annual race. We heard the swish of their tires and loud conversations about the beer they would enjoy after the race and about the upcoming hill that would be a challenge. Many of them wave to us on the porch and call out good morning. From this porch we have observed the small moments of daily life - the neighbour from up the road that walks her small scruffy dog every morning; the farmer from next door that drives his tractor up and down the road, fetching bales of hay, fetching manure, fetching soil, fetching cows to move from one field to another. The pair of chipmunks that chase each other, tails poking up in the air, across our lane and up into the Black Locust trees; the neighbour that leads his mild and serene Guernsey up to the milking shed and back again in the mornings - steaming buckets of milk in his hands; the family of blue jays that have raucously raised their young on our land this summer; the neighbour that toils in her garden, her ever attentive Border collie laying in wait outside the fence. We wave at every car and truck and tractor that passes our porch. More likely than not, they waved at us first.

There is an art of porch. The art of the front porch is to understand that it is much, much more than an architectural feature of a house. It is a place - a place to pause, and to watch, and to simply be.

DUST & LOVE ON A COUNTRY ROAD

On walks on the country roads around Fat Hummingbird Farm I look for certain places, notable markers of my foot journey. The marshes that border our country road further up, trickle and chortle with the sound of unseen springs that come down from the mountain. Red wing blackbirds sing on the tufted and exploded bulbs of bull rushes. The wood turtle finds quiet escape in the waterfall landscape feature of a neighbour's property. There are crooked fences broken and slumped in fields and meadows, their original purpose long forgotten. There is a common feature of fence corners standing alone, far out in fields, supporting nothing within their triangular presence. There are so many, many old and sometimes ancient orchards; so old I believe they have forgotten where the farmhouse was, where the barn leaned in the corner. Along our road, I come across apple trees tumbled together in brakes and thickets that must once have meant the presence of a farmhouse and an orchardist - nothing left of either but a stone foundation for one and a gravestone for the other.

It is a wonder beyond exploration when I walk our country roads - in this place where I have found my footing and lost my heart. A country road is a fulfillment in solitude, a silence, a place where memories come and you must catch them before they evaporate; where hopes are mulled on. Walking on a country road is somewhat like walking in a dream. You don't quite know who you are. As you walk along, the cows in the pasture watch you silently - their jaws working on that inevitable cud. Further along the horses in *that* field lift their tails and trot to the other end of the field, their eyes rolling suspiciously. In the next field the sheep pointedly ignore you. At the next farmhouse the chickens in the front yard scratch and squawk, the dog barks with a wagging tail, and the small child on the swing waves at you and calls "Watch me!" as she pumps her legs to get higher. You are a strange, anonymous human, one among all.

Up the road, I pass the dairy. Listening to the milking machines and the slow munch of the cows in their stanchions is tranquilizing. There is an odd, though comforting, mammal-ic sisterhood I feel with all those lactating animal spirits in one place. They snuffle with damp noses. There is a diaphanous sort of steam that hangs above the herd - made up of warm bodies, damp manure, and the heavy wetness of milk.

There are vineyards along our country road. A vineyard is the epitome of hope. All those dreams and aspirations vested in a vining plant and its small bulbous fruit. The vineyards crawl up the side of the mountain in regimented rows, facing south for the heat of the sun and the kinder winds. They grow on belief. An early frost like we had just this week can spell disaster - or ice wine.

You don't walk on country roads for exercise. Well, I suppose you could but that is not really the purpose of a country road; not if you are seeking its essence, its quality. Besides, moving aside for the bulk of various farm machinery, the occasional car with its waving passengers, or the school bus means that walking a country road is a herky-jerky business.

And walking a country road at night is yet another wonder. You must use a flashlight or a lantern. There are no streetlights at all along our road. If the moon is full then perhaps you can walk without a light. Starlight alone, though there is a literally dizzying number of them, is not sufficient for illumination. What keeps you safely on the road is the peeping of frogs, accentuated here and there with the deep throaty croak of a bullfrog. They are in the ditches either side of the road. Keep yourself in the middle of choruses and you walk true.

You know, there is a saying that when we are in love, we walk. I don't think it matters if you are in love with the road in the country or with each other - it's the being in love that matters. Country roads just provide the romance.

WOODS, DOOR, & WHISPERS

A large portion of Fat Hummingbird Farm is a woods that climbs up the side of North Mountain. It forms a dense and impenetrable border of trees and brush and knotweed that, during this first summer of our experience of this wood, is crammed with vegetation and wildlife. We have seen porcupines munching greedily high up in a tree and snakes slithering off to the brush in the glissade manner peculiar to snakes. Signs of deer and their trail-making - ripples in the tall grass, and scat of the coy-wolves we hear carolling at night. The woods carry a particular sound as the winds from off the Bay of Fundy come up and over the mountain and sheer down through the trees. It is a water-less waterfall sound - a rushing, a whorling sound of wind heaving and tugging leaves in its wash.

I have not known woods like this since my childhood in England. If I close my eyes and stand in our woods, that childhood wood returns to my senses. The summoning of a 'whole' wood, an ambience of wood-darkness, wood-silence, punctuated with the notes of birds and the paint-dab of wild flowers. Of the leaves crumbling inexorably to death. I had become habituated to the woods of the Northwest, on the west coast. There, the woods are evergreen, shaded, with a dripping dampness that feels cave-like. And quiet, too, like a cave. The scent is that of earth, and mushrooms, and moss. The deciduous trees in *our* woods are soft-leaved and carry that inevitable death within themselves. Even in the heat of summer they hear the murmurs and sighs of autumn. Their branches and their roots know - a deep knowledge of things that a tree that is forever green and never relinquishes life can never know. The scent of these woods is acrid and a bit bitter, and you can taste pollen and dust on your tongue.

As we have been clearing brush and making (very slow) headway into the woods, we have found wild apple trees, peach trees, trees that carry a berry that even the birds won't touch, and voluminous drifts of Kicking Colt (jewelweed), Goldenrod, Tatarian Asters, and numerous wild roses. In those parts of the woods we have not yet been able to access, at least not until winter, there can be seen dark portals, tenebrous shadows between the papery silver of the birches, to places unseen. They put me in mind again to the woods of my childhood; and the portals and thin places and things unseen. My Nana, on mornings that followed a summer night-time rain, would take me to the kitchen window that looked onto the woods that bordered the lower garden. There she would point out the rings of toadstools that had sprung up under the oak trees overnight.

"Fairy rings", she would say, "Look closely, look closely, can you see the fairies teasing that hedgehog?"

And perhaps as a result of her holding my arm tightly, meanly, until I replied; or as a result of her insistent, whispering, tobacco-scented voice; or as the result of my staring and staring until there were tears in my eyes and the image of the toadstools swam in and out of focus - I saw the fairies. Pointy-faced, sharp of nose and long of fingers. Their wings were honed, bony, and web-veined like shattered glass. They were not the fairies of children's books.

My Nana put out a nightly bowl of bread scraps softened with warm milk to appease these creatures of the woods. I feel the creatures of *my* woods may be gentler, more tender, kinder to me than was my Nana. I wouldn't be remiss, though, to start putting out those nightly milk sops. It would be wise . . . I think.

LOVING MONSTERS*

There is a story that claims that the wolf was put late in the procession onto Noah's Ark. That he was a creature not to be trusted. That he was not true nor faithful. That he was a monster that was to be degraded. Such is the stuff of Red Riding Hood. Over the course of this summer, late at night past midnight or in the early hours of three am, the crickets chirr to a halt and the night chorus of the coywolves begins. It starts with murmurs and ascends into hysterical yips and yaps, and finally rounds into full-throated howls that make your heart thud. There is nothing like laying in bed under civilized bamboo sheets and feeling the responsive tingle that begins in your toes and exits through the top of your head - your body and mind on a high tension wire plucked by the wild sounds. Nocturnal laments. Lunar lullabies.

When first we heard them we thought - coyotes. But the sound was not solitary nor soprano like that of the prairie coyote of our experience. As the sound became that of multiple beings and the tone deepened to mournful long howls we thought - wolves. Then neighbouring farmers told us of the coywolf - a large hybrid coyote/ wolf (sometimes mixed with dog), that has become common to the area around Fat Hummingbird Farm.

They come down from the mountain behind us and up from the valley to run the moon paths across the fields or along the trails where the railway tracks have been pulled up. The sound of them echoes off the basalt walls of the slope; we sometimes find scat in the yard close to the house; and on our walks after a rainy night we find their enormous paw prints in a disused road. When they sing their night-time canticles, the local dogs whine and call out over the wind themselves. They sense the wild. It calls to them and, if they are chained, they pull at their tethers, feeling that same wire that I feel, vibrating in their bones and blood. Dogs can be full of heartache and poetry too and dream of running with a throng.

I know, in my human scientific mind, that coyotes and wolves and our resident coywolves do not actually howl at the moon. They will ululate and keen whether there is a moon out or not. But I know of a wolf that missed the moon. He lived his entire life in a zoo. His enclosure was concrete, the bars were heavy and rusted, and at night he was shut away in a roofed ghetto where not a single glint of starlight fell through the cement ceiling, let alone moonbeams. Every weekend of my childhood living in that city I went to the zoo and sat by the wolf's cage. He was already very old. The keeper loved to tell all who would listen about the oddity of this wolf - he never howled. Not ever.

That wolf lived to be 27 years old. Never howled. Never followed nor sang along a lane of light. The keeper boasted of how it was the fact that the wolf was captive that he lived so long. That if he had been left wild he would have died after a short life. I think, maybe, lives of misery and restlessness seem to be long lives. Lives of bliss are short.

I remember another experience of wolves. We were camping with our small sons and good friends, waiting for a meteor shower; so we were up very late, high in the mountains, with only the night sky for illumination. Around our camp the darkness was deep, and beside our camp the river ran heavy and turbulent; our ears so acclimated to the sound of it running to the ocean that it was mere ambience.

Laying on our backs, we waited for the meteor shower. We guessed at what was a planets what was a star, what was a satellite spinning endlessly until it died.

Sputnik. Asteroid. Moon.

The meteorites began streaking across the night-fallen sky. One, then two, then twenty. Then, uncountable. They spoke. The fizzle of a flame. The swish of ladies' skirts. The sibilance of snakes. The whisper of vast rocks dying in the sky.

And out of the woods came the shadows of wolves. We sat up alertly - my youngest son clasped to my breast, his eyes wide and luminous in the dark. The pant-gutter sound of pursuit. The innuendo of foot-falls. The murmuring secret of them. My sons barely breathed. I felt the fluttering tremble of my youngest son's heart as he leaned back against me. It went from his chest, through his back, to my chest. Like that high tension wire, plucked and thrumming - tingling, a shiver. They stood, just for a moment, and looked our way. The gold-flecked feral yellow of wolves' eyes in the moon-soaked night. And, just for a moment - with tumbling river, and sizzling skies, and silent taciturn forest about us . . . . we were wild too.

I think of that sometimes when I lay in bed at night, listening, and I think of that moon-starved wolf too. It doesn't matter if they are coyotes, or wolves, or coy-wolves. What matters is that they know how to find the wakes left by moonlight . . . and how to sing the untamed notes of the truly wild.

* A version of *Loving Monsters* was published in Sky Island Journal, Issue 7, Winter 2019.

THE HYMN OF WOOD SMOKE

The mornings are foggy now and it takes longer and longer to burn off the mist. Crisp autumn apples are falling from the trees. It is fascinating to pick them up off the ground and see the interesting and intricate patterns insects have traced through the skin. The skies, now, are often vaporous and clouds of different sorts inhabit the sky at the same time; all of them scudding across the horizon.

Over the last few weeks we have seen heaps of firewood piled in neighbour's lanes and yards, waiting for the rhythm and order of stacking. I always feel drawn to touch the cut faces of the logs. To bend over and inhale deeply from their torn barks. To run my fingers over the delicately coloured veins of their exposed hearts - the lines that tell their life stories.

Now, on our walks, we smell wood smoke. Sometimes it is a sweet smell, as when burning apple wood. Sometimes the smell pinches at your nose - the acrid smoke of birch or pine. Sometimes the smell reminds me of the sweet, sage-like tobacco my father smoked in his pipes. A smell that still, when I sense it, makes me turn and expect to see him. Though he is gone now.

When I see the smoke coiling in loops and ringlets up from stone chimneys, I inhale large, wanting to pull the smoke deep into my lungs; to have the warm haze of it curl at the bottom of my gut. I long for my hair to smell of it so that another, lover, can draw in the heated and poignant extinction of a blazed life.

Humans are drawn innately to a wood fire. It probably stems from our ancient beginnings and the fire that kept us safe and warm and predators at bay. Good grief, there is even a TV channel that shows nothing but a burning fire all day long, with a human arm occasionally reaching in to change the position of the log. People turn that channel on at Thanksgiving and Christmas time - the times that we gather together.

What it comes down to is that we want that capering flame and the sound of crackling fire. We want that lingering, smouldering smoke smell in our clothing and our hair. It goes well with a glass of full-bodied red wine or a short glass of amber whiskey. And perhaps a cat forming his body to our lap.

We don't ourselves, at Fat Hummingbird Farm, have a wood-burning stove. Two of them were removed from the house when it was renovated prior to our buying it. Nonetheless I want the routine of wood being dumped in the driveway. I want the routine of stacking the wood - perhaps in some elaborate Norwegian style. I want the routine of piling the wood in the stove before retiring for the night. The routine of lighting it in the chill of the morning, along with the boiling of the water for coffee and the popping of bread into the toaster. I want the cat to find the lure of a warm hearth in front of the bright-burning fire.

When I smell the smoke that drifts in the air from the wood stoves of others up and down our road, I think perhaps a wood-burning stove may come to live with us. Actually, I am sure of it. And then I can watch those lives etched on the log faces, burn and blur and become souls.

RED DIRT GIRL*

Here at Fat Hummingbird Farm there are no flower gardens . . . as such . . . yet. When we arrived in mid-June drifts of lupins of numerous colours adorned the ditches up and down our road, tramped up rises and gathered in the natural dips of meadows and pastures. As the summer progressed other wild flowers of various ilk came and went and we have never been without colour, and the diversity has been remarkable. And I will always keep those spaces for those wild flowers to revisit year after year. But now it is time to put my own Monet- and O'Keeffe-inspired imprint on the landscape.

So the flower gardens begin. My husband, Bar, has been digging beds for me and, in the process, has discovered a lot of the basalt rock origins of our North Mountain and that the roots of Black Locust trees love to roam and ramble and argue over staying in certain areas where we would rather they not be. But the soil is basically pretty good, predominantly red, and in need of earthworms. I stand barefoot in the red soil and ponder 'what' plants and 'where' plants. Spiders crawl between my toes. Bar says I could be the Red Dirt Girl of song - specifically that song of Emmy Lou Harris'. But the song is sad. I like the first few lines though:

Me and my best friend Lillian
And her blue tick hound dog Gideon
Sittin' on the front porch coolin' in the shade
Singing every song the radio played . . . [1]

Hmmm, I could love a blue tick hound dog named Gideon.

Over the last of the summer and now into the autumn I have been slipping bulbs and infant perennials into that red dirt. The names of the plants themselves are a poem –

bowman's root (also known as Fawn's Breath, a name to catch
my breath),
star grass, hive vine, stork bill, butter and eggs (toadflax),
brodiea (cluster lilies), seep spring, Indian paintbrush,
olive, fig, bird's eye, goat's beard, tidy tips (platyglossa),
owl's clover, desert lantern, red birds in a tree (crimson figwort)

. . . and Kintzley's Ghost, a climbing honeysuckle once thought to
be lost forever but found again growing on the grave of the man that
developed it. Every garden needs a ghost - one that will sleep around
the plants' roots during the day and stir the flower heads at night.

I like to say the names in a chant, the words spilling off my tongue
like melodies. Like singing those songs the radio plays. I slip them into
the soil - the melodies, the plants. I feel, as I pull soil over the breast-
shaped bulbs, nipples erect, and around the tender stems of the perennials,
that I will be embodied in these gardens.

I remember the enchanted gardens of my childhood. Gardens where
the colours seemed brighter. Where I could delight in chasing butterflies
by day and fireflies by night. Gardens where the very air was clear as
our spring water and mornings moist and fragrant like our fog-draped
sunrises. Where the rhubarb was sweeter because it was stolen from
the McCafferty's garden under a nickel-silver moon. My breath-held
tension as I moved aside the loose board and bellied up to the rhubarb
patch while Mr. McCafferty smoked on his back porch - his fat, deaf
Basset Hound at his feet. The smoke of his cigarette drifted up and
curled round the single yellow lightbulb, befuddling the moths already
intent on a death of wing-sizzling immolation. Smothering the crack-
crackle noise of the breaking stem with the hem of my dress, I would
tear one piece of rhubarb for me and another for my brother, waiting in
the alleyway with sugar in a twist of foil in his pocket. Sometimes I also
stole Mrs. McCafferty's tulips to give to my mother, or crushed the
petals of her spicy/sweet roses and smeared them on my wrists as
perfume.

Thus far *these* flower gardens are a leap of faith. Though the autumn chill will reduce the perennials to dry leaf and stark woody stems, and the winter snow will lull the bulbs into a bear-like hibernation, I know the spring will be an awakening. I will feel embodied in the budding blooms and the bright green impertinence of the bulb shoots cracking the soil as the winds warm. The flowers will eat light and grow strong. The soul of these gardens will run like sap in my veins, blended with the blood. Like a rose of red, pushing its thorns and roots through my heart, out of my toes into the soil. I feel it would not be untoward, on a future spring night, to lift my face to a full moon and bay, under the wide-open stare of a midnight owl.

I know these gardens will witness me. Acknowledge me. As the breeze dances through the golden nodding heads of the Kintzley's Ghost, I may dance in my gardens with naked, dirty feet. On the red dirt. With a blue tick hound named Gideon.

---

[1] Red Dirt Girl by Emmylou Harris

* A portion of this essay appeared in *'Star Grass & Bowman's Root'*, published in Sky Island Journal, Issue 2, Fall 2017

STREAMS: LOST & WILD

Everything is flowing somewhere. Glaciers, and avalanches, and dirt down a mountainside, and air, and animal migrations. And water. Rivers. Streams.

The first stream I remember playing in we weren't supposed to be playing in. My mother had sent my brother and me out to play, out onto the face of the prairie on a cold, sub-zero winter's day. We had tired of sledding and making snow angels and hiked out into the coulees. My brother, smaller and younger than me, was struggling with the deep snow. I told him to walk in what appeared to be a rut, where the snow seemed less deep. In he stepped, and in he sank, into a stream hidden beneath the snow. At first I worried that he would drown . . . but the water only came up to his waist. Then I worried that he would freeze. I hauled him out of the stream and stripped his clothes and boots from him. While he shivered and turned a frightening shade of white/blue, I upended the boots and emptied them; wrung out his clothes. Then I redressed him with the addition of my scarf in one boot and my mitts in the other and my extra layer of sweater wrapped around him. We trudged home numb and beyond cold. Then I worried that he would tell my mother. He never did.

Another stream I remember was also a prairie stream. We were older now. We were staying at a friend's farm. My brother and the three sons who lived there went to the stream to catch tadpoles. The tadpoles numbered in the hundreds and the boys would bring home great mason jars of them that they left in the hot sun on the porch rail - soon forgetting about their captives in that careless cruelty that small boys engender. The water got murkier as the day's heat bore on and the tadpoles swam slower and slower. The daughter and I would wait until the right moment then fetched a wagon while the boys were busy with something else. We loaded up all the mason jars of infantile frogs and hauled them back to the stream. There we freed them into the bubbling water. They floated and bobbed about, having us think that we had waited too long. Then suddenly they whipped their sperm-like tails, right themselves and scurry away - as though the stream had made Lazarus' of all of them, bringing them back from the dead.

Before we moved here to our farm we lived in a suburban area bordering on the city. There the streams flowed beneath the streets. They are called 'lost' streams. Streams are characterized in environmental reports as either wild, threatened, endangered, or lost. The ones that are lost are those that have been built or paved over but still continue to flow in the subterranean depths beneath the neighbourhoods. Landscapes eclipsed by development. Streams lost and forgotten. The streams remember though:

"Listen; the buried stream gurgles its longing to return to daylight and moonlight: to nourish ducks, bracken, ferns, salmonberry, and newt; to live." ~ Anon

It makes me deeply sad to think of lost streams, like Peter Pan's lost boys running through the forests, looking to be found. I imagine those lost watercourses yearn to be wild.

Here at Fat Hummingbird Farm we have a stream. It has been quiet most of the summer. I feared we had lost it, though there has obviously been enough incipient moisture to keep peeper frogs happy and singing, and even the occasional sonorous bullfrog. It is fall now, though, and the stream has reappeared, running strong enough to chortle over stones. The stream bed is quite deep and I have been told that in the spring that stream will be a torrent.

Over our stream there is a wooden bridge. And nailed to a tree beside the bridge is a sign that says 'Max's Bridge'. Max is the grandson of the former owners of our farm. From what we have been told this Max is a precocious, fairly wild child. The stories of him remind me of that child Max that appeared in Maurice Sendak's book *Where the Wild Things Are*. The Max in *that* story misbehaved and was sent to bed with no supper. So he ran away to an imaginary island where he became the King of the Wild Things. Let the wild rumpus start!

Wild boys, wild streams. I love that our stream is wild and not lost. I love that the bridge was named for a wild child. I love that the stream has come back to sing full-throated. And though we have no Max living with us the sign on our bridge will be staying. To signify a wild child sitting on a bridge, swinging his legs, over a wild stream where the tadpoles wriggle their butts and swim to the river.

DARK*

People do not always understand that darkness is a gift. We never knew dark before we came to Fat Hummingbird Farm. Not really. Not *real* dark. The occasional camping trip or venture out to a party in the country gave us a taste. But we had never really 'lived' dark.

In the suburbs of our previous lives the dark of night was always polluted with light. Streetlights, the yard lights of the train yard, the sign lights from the motel just over the block. The general constant glow of the city as a whole that lifted above like an umbrella. Dark was never really dark. You could always see your way on a late night walk or out to the backyard to see where the dog had ventured.

Here, on the farm, dark is an essence. Here you can watch the dark rise just like you watch the sun rise in the mornings. It starts out the window of our east-facing guest bedroom. It rises up and over our house and our mountain, pulling its bruised-blue, then deepening purple-black cape behind it. Shrouding us. It lumbers on west, the various lights of day winking out behind it. We often take the cue from that bedroom window and hurry to the yard where we can watch our hayfield and willow trees darken behind our former barn and disappear into night.

Here, we have a deeper understanding of dark. Unlike in the city where darkness is hinted at around the haloed glow of lamplight, dark at the farm is substantial and genuine. It is so much more than just the simple absence of light. Dark strokes your skin. It nudges itself under the fall of your hair, questing at the nape of your neck, drifting down your shoulders. It glides into your mouth, onto your tongue, down into your lungs. It creeps behind your eyes and slips into your mind. You see dark differently.

Even as a child I preferred dark, preferred night. Darkness softens the barbed edges of day; it tones down the too often strident colours of bright-lighted day. With the coming of dark, rather than the world closing in, the universe seems to expand. There is so much promise in dark. The world as a whole seems to feel that. The shapes of things become obscured and blurred. The objects become the essences of themselves, slink back into their own nature. Become . . . absolution.

But let me be clear, dark is not necessarily black. At night, when I look to our pasture the darker lumps of cows can still be seen moving slowly across the field, doing whatever mysterious thing it is that cows do at night. Or the shadow of some kind of night bird - owl, whippoorwill, nightjar - moves to a tree branch like a drift of smoke. Those trees can be seen as a darker shade against the night canvas. And if the moon is out . . . well then the land is awash with silver, pearl against black. And the dark takes on the ornate finery of a monochromatic costume party. Nacre dresses and ebony masks. And the round hay bales wear the silver backs of grizzlies.

The dark in the country means that we have seen Venus in the sky every single night. It shines bright and low even on the cloudiest night. Jupiter has also made an appearance most every night and, on one night during the summer, hung close to Venus along with a cuticle-shaped moon. The stuff of post cards. Other occasional planets, or satellites, or a star dying with more ardent passion than usual, make pinprick tracks across the night sky like ambient fireflies.

Back in the city, dark was something you put up with until the brightness of day came and you went on with your busy lives. Here, you wear the darkness. Hold it close and breathe in its night-time breath glorious with the smell of wet frogs and sleeping trees. Listen to its whispering poems of night winds and canny foxes. Taste the dark like moss and spring water on your tongue.

---

* A version of *'Dark'* was published in Sky Island Journal, Issue 11, Winter 2020.

WIND DANCES THE TARANTELLA

'Wutherin' is a term that my Grandad, long ago, used to describe the wind that sometimes built up on the moors above his wee farm. The kind of wind that rushes and blusters and thumps at doors and windows. A hollow shuddering, a yawning roar. As I sit writing this the wind is wutherin' at the windows and doors at Fat Hummingbird Farm. The last couple of weeks have seen wind storms that shake the windows, bend the willows to their knees, and knock birds head over tail feathers in the air. The clearing behind the house is strewn with branches and twigs of all sizes - some probably not even our own but blown from neighbours. And an old dead tree that I have grown to love over the summer, its whitening branches and trunk bedecked with a colourful ivy, has fallen. The roar of the wind is fairly constant and, at night especially, the wind bawls and beats the house with a variety of knocks and thuds and rasps that leads you to believe that it doesn't like being out in the dark either and would love to come in. Last night the wind whimpered and whined and scratched in a way that sent my husband outside looking for what we were sure must be a frightened and lost dog.

I grew up on the Prairies and there, rather than the occasion of a wind storm, the wind blew almost constantly. It was an uninterrupted tug - at your clothing, at your face - buffeting at your ears and blowing your wind-tattered hair almost from your scalp. Its wild thrust through wheat fields and tall prairie grasses was as insistent as the waves plunging up the shores of the Bay of Fundy. Its pitch was higher and it always sang lonely. Always.

Out west there the wind almost always blew in one direction - once it decided what direction that was. It was not in the habit of changing its mind and shifting course. Here at Fat Hummingbird Farm the wind most often gallops down North Mountain. But, with these wind storms, the wind careens from north to south then east to west, swirls in on itself in tight eddies, blows down to the ground then up a tree to the sky again. It is like a maddened cat with a firecracker tied to its tail. And just as spitting mad. Or perhaps one could say it dances the equally maddened pace of a tarantella - grabbing the pendulant arms of the willow and whirling them into a frenzy.

There are so many sorts of wind:

bise, mistral, bora, brickfielder, southerly buster, buran, sirocco, khamseen, gibli, xlokk, fohn, chinook, moazagoatl, zoned, saloon, etesians, shamal, trade winds, tehuantepecer, williwaw, willy-willy . . .

and of course Newfoundland's Wreakhouse wind.

There is a beautiful description of winds in Michael Ondaatje's *The English Patient* that I have always savoured reading over and over – "let me tell you about winds . . . ". Painters Monet and Gauguin both painted the Mistral wind, a strong cold northwesterly wind that blows from southern France into the Gulf of Lion in the northern Mediterranean.

The wind that is, at this moment, wutherin' at the doors and windows of what is proving to be our very solid house, does not have a fancy name - a name that invokes charm or mystery or even a kind of voodoo. But this wind is an artist, a painter - plastering forms and shapes and light upon our windows, finding expression for its wild bluster.

OF SNAW AND FEEFLE AND KATTY-CLEAN-DOORS*

The first snow of the season at Fat Hummingbird Farm and it is wild, wicked, and deep. It fell in a 'flukra' - a Scottish word for snow falling in large flakes; then turned to 'kramsno', Swedish for 'press-snow' meaning a heavy wet snow you can press together. It came accompanied by an unrelenting wind that buffets the birds mercilessly. What we sometimes think is smoke on the horizon is snow squalls - or 'snorok', a Swedish word meaning snow smoke. The squalls blow up into the trees making them appear to have a hazy foliage. Or they swirl about the cows in the pasture like cats wrapping themselves about their legs. I find myself constantly looking out of various windows to watch how the undulating shapes of the snowdrifts are being continually re-sculpted by the wind. Or to judge how the birds are faring, desperately clinging to suet cakes or bird feeders, their wings flapping rapidly to keep their precarious place on the icy-slick feeder or tray. Or to pity the cows in our pasture, their backs against the wind, their heads down and determined - the wee calves in the middle of the herd of bulky bodies.

Where we have come from on the West Coast snow is infrequent. And when it does snow, the snow turns ugly rather quickly. The whiteness turns to car exhaust-coloured black and grey. The consistency turns to slush and piles up along the curbs and in driveways creating an urban texture that is unpleasant. The sposh and sludge and slop of citified snow.

I will not romanticize snow here. The farmers in the neighbourhood have had their daily work quadrupled by frozen water, cows and chickens caught in snow up to their chests, and having to feed said cattle more often to keep them warmer. But, despite the inconvenience, the power outages, the slick roads, and the decidedly unimpressed and miserable cows out in the pastures, I realize I have missed snow.

I am not a skier or anything of the ilk that would have me waiting excitedly for snow such that I can get out there and ski, or sled, or snowshoe, or skate or whatever else people do in the snow for 'fun'. No, I have missed the ambiance of snow. The mood, the spirit of snow.

Like in the morning when you wake to a nightfall of snow. Before even looking out the window you know snow has fallen. There is a profound hush. The world inhales and forgets to exhale. It holds its breath. Everything *watches* - the jackrabbit, the porcupine, the fox shuffling slippered feet across the tops of crystalline drifts.

The bare lines of the trees and the denuded tangles of low brush - the bone yard results of the autumn winds stripping the colour and the leaves - are now accentuated. But drifts of snow in crevasses and along branches, knotted and twisted in plump shapes, re-soften the lines, giving the plants a new foliage to wear. The snow piled at the feet of the trees is peppered with the bedroom slipper tracks of jackrabbits and the sharp pen etchings of bird tracks.

The wind sounds different when there is snow. It speaks differently in this scape. It doesn't carry birdsong or the constant buzz of cicadas or the chortle of the stream like it does in other weather. It carries, instead, the shushing sound of wind polishing snow to an icy glaze. Or it carries the deep moan that sings the cold. Or the sound of my steps crunching - like snapping peanut brittle. Or, as the result of snow piled high and heavy on mere twigs, the sound of the cracking fracture from the tree limb like a leg in a trap.

When colour has been snow (white)-washed, when sound has been muted, when the light is callous and stabbing - bouncing from the stark hoariness, one must look for a distinct kind of beauty, a singular kind. That spare-ness, that simplicity, lays everything exposed. My sight expands. There is nothing to see but the blunt, sheer truth of a thing, of a place. And if I am lucky, on a snow-wrapped black evening, I may see an owl - more silver than the snow, turn her head and peer. Blink.

Scottish words for snow, swirling snow, and a child's word for snow.

MARE'S TAILS & COLT'S BREATH

I am fond of the sounds of horses. Sometimes throughout the day I will hear them neigh or nicker from distant fields. I love how, at night, one can wander through a stable and you can hear the slow munch of feed, the lifting of a hoof, the swish of a tail, a stamping of metal shoe on wooden floor. I love how, when you stand next to a horse, perhaps your forehead pushed into their neck, how the air *tastes* of horse.

My first experience with horses was in England when I was very small. A neighbour of my Grandad's had two or three little retired pit ponies. They were blind and rather moth-eaten and very ill-tempered. My Grandad would plonk me down on the back of one and away it would go! I was sort of like those poor kids that hang on for dear life to the backs of sheep at rodeos. It was only a matter of time until the pony tossed me over a fence or into a ditch or simply stopped, its little legs rigid and back humped, while I sailed over its head and into the inevitable puddle or cowplop. I loved it! I would beg my Grandad over and over again to put me back on the pony so I could "ride".

My love for horses, even with such an inauspicious beginning and with such a puny and crotchety 'horse', was imbedded deep in my fibre. I had my own horse eventually. My father won him in a poker game. That's a whole other story but suffice it to say that that horse had a great deal in common with the acerbity of the pit ponies.

My Grandad also had a draft horse - a Percheron I think it was. One summer he was using the horse to attempt to pull out a large stump. It was a huge, stubborn stump that had tangled its searching roots deep into the earth and stone in just the place that my Grandad wanted to extend his garden. The horse hauled all summer at that stump. The stump was steadfast and tenacious. So was the horse. My job was to wipe the sweating, heaving flank with a wisp of hay (though I barely reached his belly) or to hold the bucket while he took gasping gulps of water. He would nibble at the hair on the top of my head as I held the bucket beneath his nose.

The stump won, ultimately, and stayed where it was while my Grandad sought a different place for his garden. But that horse never said no; never balked at yet another day of fruitless and exhausting labour; accepted both the hearty 'good boy' slaps on his neck and the switch at the back of his legs when Grandad was frustrated. And its eyes were gentle and forgiving.

Here at Fat Hummingbird Farm, horses are plentiful on the surrounding fields and pastures. But unlike the hot-blooded jumpers and Thoroughbreds that are used for pleasure riding on the Western Coast area where we moved from, or the quarter horses and scrawny cayuses on the Prairies on which I was brought up, almost all the horses along this road are draft horses. I've never seen such a variety of draft breeds in one place!

There are three Percheron yearlings, like my Grandad's, still some time away from their eventual bulk and size. They have been in the same huge field all summer. Each time I see them they are that much taller with a bit more muscle. Then there are the Norwegian Fjord and Icelandic horses - looking even in the heat of summer like they are bracing their wide butts against cold and icy winter winds, the Clydesdales (with a foal with the too big ears and feet of a hound puppy), and the Halflingers that seem to be at several places. Another neighbour has a sizeable herd of American Creams - mares and foals, turning from creamy white to dirty and yellow brown over the course of the summer. Even the neighbour who does Dressage does it on a Canadian - his bulk not belying his ability to dance. Some use the drafts for horse-logging up the sides of our mountain. Some use them for pulling competitions or wagon hauling. Some use them for that same inexorable stump pulling. Some - well just because horses make the landscape beautiful.

There have been times in my life when an experience with draft horses has been magical. On a cold, wintry day back on the Prairies, a friend took my boys and myself to visit an old farmer he knew. A few miles north of Fort McLeod in Alberta, near the Standoff reservation. Stitching back and forth across the land from one backcountry road to another. Finally dipping down into the coulees and into a dilapidated farmyard. The man and his wife invited us into the warmth. Floors that creaked, shelves that groaned. We were served tea and stale cake

The farmer took us to see his horses. Seven. White, very large, very old horses. Bony, thin, huge feet. Draft horses of some ilk. Our friend, Jim, said this man was the last of the horse farmers in that whole area and that he and those horses had grown old together. When both the farmer and the horses were young they would plough fields and haul hay. Sometimes they would drag stones out of a field with a sledge.

They panicked at the sight of us strangers. Flared nostrils. Rolling eyes. Enclosed in a pen sloped up a muddy, stone-studded hill, they milled up and down. Galloped in circles, snorting and whinnying. Their hooves created sparks as they struck the rime-slicked stones. Like the god, Thor, with his hammer and anvil. Their forms morphed and transmuted, each with the other.

"They are ghost horses," one of my sons sighed.

And yes, ghosts swirled in the snowflakes that were just beginning to fall and in the air that eddied around these ancient horses that flew sparks from their hooves.

It started to snow harder and the horses swarmed nearer us, the steam rising from their backs. One of my sons reached his hand up to the face of one of the horses and she blew her equine breath with pink-rimmed snorts into the winter cold - and she nibbled the pom-pom of the toque on the top of his head.

THE REVELATION OF BARE BRANCHES

Fall is my favourite season. And also my favourite is hat brief undecided time that is not fall but is not yet winter. A time when the bone structure of a landscape reveals itself. Where there are stories in the 'waiting' shape of trees and woods. It is a time when there is an art of shape and shadow and tone to the trees. It is also a time that speaks to those 'thin places' - those places that are between here and there and where spirit resides. Here, on the eve of Winter Solstice, I look for the thin places that *must* exist at Fat Hummingbird Farm. This farm has abundant and good winter bones and spirit is subtly revealed.

The Black Locust trees, festooned with blossoms in the spring and pretty leaves in the summer, have a sculptural beauty in their bareness and twisted growth. The limbs look tortured and drop easily to the ground in the stiffer winter winds. The dropped limbs lay at the trees' feet. I am reminded of mouse bones and bleached grinning skulls. The branches make wonderful divining rods, apparently. As we may be seeking a well in the next year we will see if the local water witch uses the Black Locust.

The apple trees still hold red apples at the end of their contorted and whealed limbs, offering on their outstretched lines a globe of colour to the powder-shaded skies. The colour and the apple itself prevails beyond the frigid blast of winter. The Celts believed the apple is symbolic of the endurance of love and the Druids believed that eating an apple could transport one to other worlds - open one's eyes to the thin place. The tree stands as an invitation.

Some of the white birches still hold in the crooks of their branches the creeping ivy and wild rose tangle that draped them in the summer - though now the dead foliage looks like dreadlocks. Untidy and mussed but still with some of that Rastafarian thatchy endurance. Other birches, the yellow in particular, have the fine, delicate twigs at the top - greyed by the winter air and looking, from a distance, like smoke against the sky. The birch is symbolic of renewal. I expect that as the trees dress again in the spring that the accompanying ivies and roses will too.

I love the pared-back, naked and chiseled look of bare winter trees. I love the muted palettes of trunks and bark. I love how the gestural trees create shadows in the cast of winter light. Hoarfrost or snow can gather in the crooks and angles of the branches and soften the tree but in a completely different way than do summer leaves.

Winter light is softer - it opens shadows and eases highlights. The curdled texture of a winter sky is the perfect backdrop to a black and white world.

I love ice patterns on bark. I love raindrops frozen and suspended at the end of a tree's crooked finger. I love the architecture of the bare trees and the branches, and the shadows they throw, on the landscape.

I love that our willows are Goddess trees and that our oaks are considered wise.

I love that in the starkness of winter lines and winter light, long shadows and gestural shapes, the bare spirit of the tree is revealed. And I know those thin places are there - of that I am sure.

THE AUGURIES OF NIGHT

It is the heart of winter now. The cold is deep and intense, the fall of snow regular. Even the air around Fat Hummingbird Farm, with the exception of the wailing wind that comes with storms, is brightly quiet. Quiet such that when you walk past one of the Black Locust trees you can hear the crack and groan of freezing wood, the creak of a limb that may not last the winter. Their constant chatter. In the far oak, you can hear the woodpecker thud, thud, bash his insistent beak against the cold bark, hoping to catch grubs and bugs unaware in winter stupor.

These colder, leaner months bring night animals and their nocturnal doings closer to the house. They are hungry. They seek shelter. Also, the nights are longer so the world and time of the nocturnal beings has been extended and there are occasions when their protracted night-time activities and our lengthened hours of dark cross. A darker dark, an earlier dark. The world outside of our sealed windows, our locked doors, continues while we slumber.

Snow while falling masks one's passing. When it is done falling it chronicles one's passage. Most mornings now, especially if there has been even a little snowfall, tracks can be seen around the house and up into the woods. Or there are traces of tracks that imply that the creatures had come for a visit, though we were remiss in greeting them. It is an odd bewitchment in that morning to see the trace of something that was there, that was awake, that sniffed our windows and scratched at our doors, that was close - so close, while we slept the night away. And leaving those tracks, those subtle fragments of what and who they are.

The tracks of our neighbour's feral barn cat are fairly obvious. The direction from which they come and where they go is predictable. His small, neat and tucked paw prints come from the barn and across our hay field. He comes across the bridge and then slinks around the entire perimeter of the house. He comes up and onto the porch where the bird feeders hang in hopes of finding a fallible bird asleep in a place too low. His tracks continue up the hill, down and across the stream, and back to his manure- and hay-warmed barn - in time for his early morning pan of steaming milk from the dawn-milked cows.

The other day when I went to fetch the mail, early in the morning and after a night-time snowfall I saw the tracks of a fox. She had come up from the old railway tracks, across our pasture, and into the dooryard. Her tracks presented a determined gait. She didn't seem to wander but trotted resolutely up the hill and back into the woods. She may already have had prey hanging from her jaws. Or she may have felt she was already late back to her den.

There are tracks of a very large-footed hare. It seems he must pause and look about a lot, then bounds in long, long vaults. His tracks always visit the lumber pile. It so happens that my large ceramic hare resides near that lumber pile. Bleached white from the sun and the rain, with tall ears, and a bemused expression - perhaps his wild counterpart is looking for companionship, or recognized in him another moon-gazing hare. Or he is fixed on a ley line - shivering.

And there are sometimes tracks of deer. The deep divots their hooves leave are sedate and dainty and very carefully placed. Creeping reserved and reticent even under cover of darkness. There are other tracks, and brushings, and long drag-like mark's in the snow that must indicate a lower-bellied creature - a mink perhaps or a weasel.

Whatever the morning brings, with its signs and traces and auguries in the tracks of those callers, it is indisputable that a terrene 'becomes' while we hover insensible in deep sleep in ours. And that may be solace or it may be disquiet - to live with a world that just edges with ours. Where we are not the ones that leave the tracks.

MUSIC . . . AND THE LOVE OF A POET

A song courses around my head, ricocheting from ear to ear. It isn't just a melody, a run of notes. It is a touch, a quickening. As I walk our country road, I hum - bone-deep hums. Once in awhile I will sing a single line of something, from somewhere. I never know what my pace or my meandering mind will pull to my lips. It could be about hot desert highways, or dust in the wind, or the love that was deep for a Mexican maiden. I'm old - I know a lot of songs. Music evokes memory - it can pluck at your heartstrings like a cello player. There have been many scientific studies as to why that is so and I am sure they are all valid and true in their deductive way. But the why really doesn't matter to me. I just want to follow the will of my heart and my memories and go where they want to take me.

This . . .

It's a rainy Sunday afternoon. My father sits in the living room playing his records on the stereo. His foot taps and, once in a while, his fingers snap. But he doesn't sing along. Never. He likes Marty Robbins - a country singer who was also a NASCAR driver and Connie Francis and Patsy Cline. And Dean Martin, whose drunken charm and flirting style he likes to emulate. I am allowed to pull the record delicately from its sleeve and to place it carefully on the turntable. I am never allowed to drop the needle. Any smudges from my fingertips are required to be buffed off with spit and my father's handkerchief.

This . . .

My husband is a radio show host when we meet. His show is late - midnight to seven, he plays whatever he wants. He has eclectic tastes and a good ear. Listening to his provocative late-night radio voice is what I fall asleep to - hoping to hear a dedication to dream on. He plays classical music and promotes local rock bands, playing them as much as he can. We inherit the house we live in on the prairies from a rock and roll musician. He sings in the basement. Three rock bands attend our wedding. A lot of wild hair in the wedding photos

This . . .

My boys are still small. My husband is away for a long period of time and the boys and I spend a lot of time during his absence at the farm of friends. The long evenings are brimming with music and saunas and hard apple ciders. We leave after midnight in the early still dark hours of the morning to drive back into town - the boys wrapped in blankets in the back seat, smelling of horse and dirt and sauna-drenched birch. The highway is flat and dark and deserted and inevitably lit by a full prairie moon. Sometimes, as we drive along, antelope bound along in the fields beside the car, their shadows leaping at the moon. We play the radio full volume and sing along to Roxy Music or the Eagles or Roy Orbison or Kansas. My eldest son calls these times our 'midnight rides'. Rebellious. Joyful. Loud.

This . . .

When we move from the prairies to the west coast we miss those same friends keenly. One day we come home tired from work, the boys still cranky from school and hunger. The light on the answering machine is blinking on and off, indicating a message. We flip the message on and from the speaker comes the skeleton of a melodic line. A penny whistle pipes and trills a lovely Irish ballad. We all four stand still and motionless and just listen, the melody filling our hearts and putting us in mind of beloved friends. The tune comes to a melancholy end and the phone is silent. Just the tune, nothing else. We know who it is. Our old friend gifting us with a memory across country-broad telephone lines. A melody brimming with his missing and his loving.

This . . .

In high school and early university years I hang about with musicians and poets. Leonard Cohen is played at every house party. His music is the backdrop and theme for virtually all gatherings (that and Iron Butterfly's In-A-Gadd-Da-Vida but that was earlier in the night). We sit, nursing cheap wine and flapping away cigarette or marijuana smoke, and listen to Cohen sing his hurting, torn thoughts written in the blood of ink. My memories of that time and music are admittedly amply wine-soaked but I do recall that all of us bare-footed, Rapunzel-haired, gypsy-dancing girls believe that we are the Suzanne that Lenny sings of in his song of that name. I am that Suzanne, that is certain, and my skin is paper thin. I am tender and completely at the mercy of poignant lines of poetry.

This . . .

That music still takes me to memories of lovers who were poets and by being so, doomed. Well, not all, I suppose. My radio-voiced husband wrote poetry - once. I remember he wrote about brown coulees and the kiss of green in spring. He wrote of a young son he felt was too emotionally fragile for this hurting world (he was right). He wrote about how the sun dappled the arm of his lover sleeping in the early morning light. And I always hoped that the lover he wrote of was me. Music and the memories that bring back tunes and words - love and fragility. Sacred rituals, whispered dedications, prairie nights filled with songs sang full-voiced out of open car windows and across stubbled fields. The music that makes poets of us; cause us to utter words about love and loss, about the vault and whorl of a coulee hill, about the curve of a lover's thigh.

I am walking now - over the land. The air is silent, still. I'm humming the Water is Wide. Because I have reached the stream.

A MURDER. A DULE, AND A PARLIAMENT

Eating breakfast at Fat Hummingbird Farm takes up most of the morning. That is due to the vast number of birds that come to the bird feeders on the porch. Two of the largest kitchen windows look out onto this porch and the feeders are hung close to them, providing unimpeded viewing. The fascination of watching the birds makes toast and coffee go on for a long time - at least until the toast has hardened and the coffee is lukewarm. We are in a kind of 'flow state' as we watch various flocks of birds come to the feeders, each at some internal time schedule that is constant enough to set a clock to if we were wont to set clocks. Crows, starlings, jays, finches, nuthatches, chickadees, pine siskin, ravens, downy woodpeckers and red-bellied woodpeckers, cardinals, the occasional birds we have not yet identified, and my beloved doves. The feeders are shared with at least two, more likely three, pairs of squirrels and last night a pair of juvenile raccoons pawed through the feeder on the table, knocked at the window, and peered large-eyed and brashly at us when we turned on the outside light.

But in the mornings a sort of meditative calm takes us over as we creep about our kitchen duties, trying hard not to startle them off with a cupboard door slammed too loudly or a sneeze. The chickadees are especially bold and tend not to fly off. The doves, on the other hand, fly off on their whistling wings at the slightest noise or motion. Just this week, though, they appear to be more accepting of our human ways and startle less, watching us warily but starting, in wee tittles, to trust.

I hope that they see we are kind. I hope that one day they will trust us like birds trust an artist friend of mine. Once, many years ago, I called far out to Ontario, to her home. Her husband answered the phone and I asked to speak to her. He took the phone with him to the kitchen window to call her, as she was outside.

"Oh!", he said, "She can't come now. She is standing out there covered in birds. They are perched all over her arms and on her head, fluttering at the ends of her fingers!"

The birds don't have to do anything particularly spectacular to have us watch so keenly. It is in the nature of their very 'bird-ness' that we are drawn to share our lives at Fat Hummingbird Farm with them. We watch the birds and forget all about the time, and indeed the world. Why? Because when they fly and flit about it is a merging of light and ebullience and colour. They are a fleetness of the moment. They do not have to have a meaning or a purpose or an explanation. The ambiance they create is simply enough to be of wonder.

Here on the Farm I am so happy that we are graced with the sweetest of birds - the mourning dove. Back on the West Coast we had doves though I never saw them. I would hear them but rarely, if ever, saw them. I am thrilled that we have a flock of at least thirty doves that call Fat Hummingbird Farm home. And they don't hide from us. Before their turn at the morning feeders they gather in the oak tree at the side of the house, looking like how partridges in pear trees are depicted on Christmas cards. Chubby. When it is their turn they swoop onto the flat trays, onto the table, or onto the driveway where Bar has scattered seed for them. Their gentle call of coooaOOOOO-woo-woo-woo greets us in the hushed quiet of the morning and calls softly into the night - just until the moon rises. It is like a solemn hymn. Many years ago, in an exceptionally stormy summer, I found several of their nests fallen to the ground. They are the frailest and most delicate nests I have seen - shallow soft bowls made of pine needles and grass stems. Even more delicate than the nests of bush tits. A group of mourning doves is called a dule - which means pitying. Perhaps I love them best because pity, though sorrowful, is also merciful. We all need mercy in our lives.

I have not seen bush tits at the farm yet. Back on the West Coast, in the summer season, great flocks of tiny bush tits descended habitually on a bush in the yard. The bush tits are *so* very tiny, like little fairy birds.

They twittered constantly as they swarmed like bees over the bush. The twittering sounds like baby breaths breathed through tiny chimes. I've come across, once or twice, their strange hanging nests made of moss and spider webs. What else but a fairy-blessed creature would make nests out of spider webs? Perhaps they will come this summer - to find us here at our home on the east coast.

Sometimes nightly, in numbers more copious than those west coast bush tits, crows crowd in the evening skies in waves and waves of discordant cacophony. They are going to trees to roost for the night, cuddled bum to beak along branches and briar. They build incredibly messy nests and chase the song birds sometimes, jealous of their melodic voices compared to their own hoarse and jangling racket. But I love crows. I admire their temerity. We have a group of about four to six that come daily to march about the yard in their self-important, Winston Churchill-esque way. They race the squirrels to rough-shelled peanuts, a favourite of both. They will sometimes spend entire afternoons sitting in the Black Locust trees imitating squeaky farm gates, a creaking branch, or a mewing kitten.

A neighbour has promised that bluebirds will come soon. And another neighbour is building a barn. He is deliberately leaving the mow door unfinished and open in hopes of attracting barn swallows. I do hope they come. A group of barn swallows is called a gulp. And I know when I see them cutting the evening light into shards with their sharp swooping wings, I gulp at the beauty of them. As the winter is warmed away other species of birds will return from their southern respites and will come to sing at Fat Hummingbird Farm.

I collect bird feathers. The feathers live in a pile of colour in a ceramic dish on a table. The feathers are like messages left in secret places where I am meant to happen upon them. Or Bar will find a feather on one of *his* walks about the farm and add it to the bowl, saying nothing, until I notice the new colour glinting in the bowl. I am always surprised at how delighted I feel to see that. And to have birds that leave messages. And to have someone who knows that I need to see them.

APRIL COME SHE WILL (WITH A NOD TO SIMON & GARFUNKEL)

Yesterday was bright, sunny, comparatively warm. Today it is raining, the wind blows hard enough to make both the trees and bird feeders dance, and it is comparatively chilly. The weather whips back and forth like reeds on the edge of wetland, blown by spring winds. Sugar weather. Our streams runs freely during the day but at dusk forms frazil, the ice crystals of turbulent weather. Such is spring at Fat Hummingbird Farm. Spring is fickle and teasing, exasperating and inspiriting. And we are thrilled! We have not seen spring, a true spring, in thirty-five years. Since we left the prairies. From that time we lived on the West Coast and though spring may be noted by the pink of the cherry blossom trees, spring is rainfully like every other season there. So, despite its contrariness and polarity, we embrace spring like the long-lost friend that it is.

It was the Spring Equinox a couple of days ago. Days now can grow longer by as much as six minutes at a time, pulling dusk and dawn closer together over a shortening night. In that shortened night sits a full moon, the Worm Moon. The smell in the air is less of snow and more of rain. The petichor - the distinct scent of rain. Or to be more precise, the scent of an oil that's released from the earth into the air before rain begins to fall. The daylight is shifting.

I am waiting impatiently for the forsythia to bloom - yellow stars and curls on bare grey branches. In the still-sleeping garden beds, waiting for the fork that turns their chilled soils up to the steaming sun, we've noticed the first Robin of the year. He hopped and waddled in search of the first spring earthworms, his chortling call a bright note in the air. The crows are starting to scavenge under the trees in hopes of material for their nests. They drag winter-fallen branches in their beaks, falling over them as they go. They underestimate the weight of those branches. Though from what I have seen of the crow nests exposed in the fall, messy and inarticulate, most have managed to get those unwieldy branches up and poked into the nests successfully.

The mornings, that have been dark and still all winter, are now cacophonous with birdsong - singing up the early sun. The birds are here in greater numbers now, and in the near midnight time I sometimes hear again the giggles and yips of coywolves. I don't realize that I've missed them until they are here again and I wonder how I went a whole winter without hearing them.

Although it will be awhile yet before the land about us turns green again and the warmth can be trusted not to disappear in a wild wind, Mother Earth is loosening winter's grip. Distending buds and embryos. Shortening the midday shadows.

Everything is careening towards growth. We humans keep fires during the winter, striving to keep cold and dark at bay. But now there seems to be a fire within the landscape itself - flowing through the trees, shattering the clouds and lighting them from within. It gives voice to new spring peepers, pulls the turtles from the chilled mud, and brings the wild down from the mountain. Already we have seen porcupines and skunks and coyotes. And there was a bear in one neighbour's field and there has been a herd of deer in another neighbour's pasture. The chirping and whistles and songs of birds is like an orchestra loudly tuning up as they croon for mates. It is the time of Gokotta - a Swedish term that means to wake up in the early morning with the express purpose of going outside to hear the first birds of spring sing.

In the same way that frozen branches of trees start to thaw in the warmth, producing sap in their lymph, my muscles and tendons long to unfold from winter's cramp. I want to stride and stretch - rather than inch over ice or slog through snow. We develop over the course of winter that same torpor seen in winter rivers and roots in our blood and our bellies, our muscles and bones. We too are frozen. I want, fervently, to walk our land. Time to find again the liminal places at Fat Hummingbird Farm. Like the one at the edge of our woods where open grass becomes shadowed and deep places. And where there is a sighing silence. Or the rocky outcrop in the middle of the field where unique plants escape the plow or the munching of cows. Or the liminal place I know exists by the edge of the stream, under the willows, where the mosses and grasses and reeds will come alive again - the moistness and relative warmth producing sheets of frog spawn. The transition place between water and land that is nothing if not fervent, fetid, and feral. A liminal place.

Spring is such a strong season. The spring winds and waters are full of elation and riot. Spring breathes into us. It breathes into us a rhythm, a deep desire, which all animals and plants understand. We *all* rise to an ascending sun.

Spring at Fat Hummingbird Farm . . . . . I am put in mind of the Irish word - Tenalach. It means the relationship one has with land/air/water, a deep connection that allows one to literally hear the earth sing. That song lightens our step so we can match the pace set by the Vernal Equinox. A joyful pace.

OF MUDROOMS & GENERAL MUCK

I have come to see that the mudroom, that ubiquitous liminal space in a home, is very much what it says it is when living in the country. Especially in spring. Especially when spring offers various kinds of wetness. And especially when your soil is clay. A place to shed the accoutrements of snow, rain, and mud and transition to the warmth and ambience of the kitchen.

In our previous city/suburban homes the 'mudroom' was merely an entryway. A space to place shoes barely dirtied by the outside world, to put son's sports equipment in varying states of stink, to hang your guests' coats and the dogs' leashes, to collect the mail and magazines and advertisement detritus that came through the mail slot. The floors were gleaming tile. A designer-like mirror hung for that last minute tidying of hair or scarf before scooting off to the office.

The closest that a previous mudroom actually served the purpose of mudroom was when we lived in an old farmhouse on the prairies. It had once sat in the middle of hectares of fields. But over time the land had been sold off in smaller and smaller packages until the old farmhouse was now a city house and sat on a 25-foot lot - hemmed in by urban lawns and houses shoulder to shoulder. The sun porch room, hanging off the front of the house and threatening for years to fall completely off, served the purpose of mudroom, slightly reminiscent of its original purpose. There our kids' bikes nested, tires tangled. Wild cats were fed and sheltered from winter storms. Muddy boots and snow-soaked socks were kicked off and left to dry to salty hardness. There was a crawl space below this room. Often in the spring you could smell the slightly-sweet smell of rotting mice carcasses that had died there over the winter or the insistent tomcat smell that stayed even after the cats had returned to the prairie in the warming weather. It was the ultimate definition of 'clutter'. A threshold. That 'brink' between outside and inside.

Here at Fat Hummingbird Farm, we once again have a real mudroom. There are hooks for coats and hats, a bench upon which to sit to wrest off mud-caked boots, a reused flower urn to hold walking sticks (it no longer holds umbrellas - an urban accessory that I learned scares cows badly and can make one stick out absurdly as a former city slicker). The mudroom has an attached bathroom to rinse off garden detritus or to throw filthy clothes in the washer, and now to house the cat's litter box. There is a mirror, *not* like the one in that suburban entryway. This one is easily removed from the wall for a quick wipe and clean after flapping one's hands dry too messily; or used to find and remove those pesky leaves and twigs that seem to delight in riding in one's hair. And the light in the mudroom bathroom is particularly bright - easier to search for those pants-clinging ticks before entering the house further.

Here in the country, the mudroom is a constant necessity. The spring rains and our hayfield that is currently a run-off bog mean that our boots are often covered in a viscous clay mud. When it dries it leaves a chalky, slippery dust on the tiles and crusty, flaking clods in the tractor-like treads of our boots. Spring snow is puddle-prone and melts quickly into small ponds about your boots, making the mudroom floor a marshland. Mud-time, mud-season, whatever it is that you want to call it, you will bring the outside inside - inevitably.

As spring gets further entrenched at Fat Hummingbird Farm the clutter increases in the mudroom. Mason bee houses sit on the bench, awaiting their placement around the farmyard. The bench is stacked with unread papers destined to be garden mulch. The hooks are draped with not one but usually at least two kinds of jackets as winter cold is not quite gone but spring warmth is not quite sincere enough to be trusted. The winter parkas and the light hoodie - both with knit hats or mittens stuffed in their pockets. The mudroom is a repository for things that don't quite fit elsewhere in the house. It is a curio cabinet of oddments and all sorts - like the long extendable claw-like picker-upper thingie that needs to be at hand but doesn't really have a place. It resides in the reused pot with the walking sticks.

Mudroom as liminal space. It snares the debris of outside before it becomes inside debris. It is the place to go it you can't find something - like the sausages that came in from the car but didn't make it as far as the refrigerator. It is the place to stop a rambunctious animal for a foot wipe before going into the house. Best of all, it is a sanctum from the weakness of trying to live spotlessly. Keep your elegant urban entryways. I need some space for the bat house before it is hung and my odd sock - the other lost in the mud.

THE LONG RAIN

It has been a very wet and very cold spring. The evening weather forecasters delight in crooning about this record or that record being broken in regard to low temperatures or high rainfall amounts. Sunny days are boring for them. They like the drama of unusual weather, the excitement of predicting the unexpected. Like Cassandra, we ignore them at our peril. The locals do say that this *is* an unusually wet and cold spring. But with all the climate change events around the world I fear that this may be a new normal.

Actually, in truth, I feel that we, ourselves, are starting to fit in to a local tradition of whinging about the weather, like all country folk do. About how the wet means you can't get tractors into the field to plant. Or that you have to now plant a different crop - one that doesn't take so long to grow. Or that our neighbour's cows were put on our pasture so late this year because the pasture was too wet. It still is. But they had run out of hay, for one. And secondly, the cows have become cranky and troublesome because they are so craving green feed. We heard the bull next door spend most of one afternoon kicking the wall of the barn that he had been cooped up in all winter, bellowing and thumping his need to get on pasture.

We are at least a month behind in building the infrastructure for our gardens and for the farm in general - let alone actually planting plants and trees and such. We have now to find more ways of controlling the water runoff from the mountain than merely using rain barrels. Now we talk of digging swales and ditches and, as a water assessor said of our hay pasture, perhaps even converting said hay field to wetland. Which would not be such a bad idea. In fact, quite laudable and certainly a boon for all the ducks and herons and turtles and frogs and snakes and birds that are in need of such wetland as more and more land gets turned into crops. But I do wish that it was a choice rather than what may be a necessity.

Each week, I wash and fold and put away the heavier sweaters and winter socks. And before the week is out they are back in circulation again. I feel like an onion, several layers worn over several layers - the layers always added, rarely taken away. I am ALWAYS cold.

Hanging laundry is somewhat of a game of cat and mouse. I sneak out and hang my laundry on the line, hoping that the sky gods do not notice and haul in the thick cumulous clouds, heavy with rain. I study the sky throughout the day hoping for enough weak sun and wind to dry and take the clothes back down before the rain falls. I don't always win, ending up drying the clothes draped over furniture in the house after all.

The hens, too, are sick of the cold and rain. They spend most of those days huddled under the pine trees, their heads scrunched down into their shoulders, alternating between standing on one cold foot and then the other. They look wet and scruffy and are the epitome of the term 'mad as a wet hen'. Their favourite dust baths places are far from dry. So instead they pick and nibble at their skin and feathers, muttering and scowling.

Frost advisories have become an evening norm. The nights still remain much too cold. Nightly, the cold creeps in under the barely open bedroom window and curls on the sill like a cat. Every once in awhile it reaches out its arctic paw and chills an exposed toe or the end of a nose. The fog that forms overnight breathes its frigid breath on the upper windows leaving them fog-licked and opaque in the morning light.

But I am truly sick of the rain and the cold. As temperatures have not risen and the threat of impending rainfall is checked compulsively on my phone app several times a day, my mood deteriorates. I know I said that having an actual spring season was something that I now loved. But even people who have lived here a good long time say that this is an unusually wet and cold spring. So I reserve the right to complain about this unusual spring.

Maybe the sun will shine tomorrow.

A CASE OF NO SIRENS ... AND A ROOSTER AT DAWN

Innumerable games of Monopoly, gathering interestingly mottled stones on the shore of the Bay of Fundy, being chased by roaring waves on the South Shore, finding the quaintness or the high artistry of local artisans and crafters, being part of a community makers' swap, watching calves play with each other in a pasture, feeding carrots to the elderly pair of mare and donkey, calling 'the girls' with the cow bell and feeding them corn, checking several times a day for the arrival of an egg, walking the old rail trail to take photos of pigs rummaging in the brush or of a cow minding her sleeping calf, playing with the cat, helping to set and clear the table for a meal, eating whole foods and trying kombucha (yuk!).

Travelling over an hour for East Indian food, gliding on the Annapolis River in an old whaler boat, seeing so *so* many cemeteries, swimming in an outdoor pool in the middle of a forest, talking to people at the farmer's market. Checking out all the unusual license plates, commenting on the lack of traffic (and also the number of road kill), helping to weed and set up a new garden, hauling stones for said garden. Trying to figure out how the hens get onto the fence to roost - they never do it when we are watching (consensus: there are only ever three on the fence - the fourth must hide the ladder). And hundreds and hundreds of photos taken with a single, old cell phone because everything is 'just so neat'.

Our grandkids have been here for the last three weeks. They are suburban kids, living in an area abutting a major, very busy and very expensive, city. We weren't sure how they would adjust to a period of time away from busyness, and constant and ubiquitous electronics, and noise. But I think they loved being here. Myself, I have felt that moving here is 'coming home'. But then I had a lot of rural experience as a kid. These two have had none of that experience. It was the little comments here and there that pointed out to me how very different life is here:

"I haven't been woken by sirens even once, Nana", says my grandson.

"People here don't call me names 'cause I'm fat, Nana. They don't even notice", says my granddaughter.

"There are no billboards on these country roads", they said - so we counted blue cars and watched for American license plates instead.

One day we passed a field with a pair of big Clydesdale draft horses in it and I told them the story of how, when I was a kid, spending summers on a farm, the draft horses were our diving boards. On hot summer days, when the chirr of the grasshoppers was at its highest and even the wind was down for an afternoon nap, we kids would go down to the river to swim. Grampa Crawford would put three or four kids on the backs of each of his big Clydesdales, slap their rears and say 'river'. Off they would amble at a slow sleepy pace, we kids on top with the first hanging onto the mane and each kid behind hanging on tightly to the one in front. We were in bathing suits and soon our legs would be rashy and itchy because of the coarse horse hair and the black flies would move from tormenting the horses' eyes to, instead, taking bites out of our bare backs and arms.

At the river the horses would clop clumsily through the muddy rocks at the edge and then move out into the current until they were up to their withers. There, they would fall asleep, their muzzles just at the water's surface; their snores causing ripples. Then we would dive from their backs into the river, bobbing and swimming about in a current that was just strong enough to cause a thrill, but not strong enough to take us more than a couple of strokes from the horses. We would use their tails to haul ourselves back up onto their backs and dive again and again into the water. The signal that we had better get back on was a loud snort from one or the other of Doug or Brew. No one ever missed this cue and got left behind in my recollection. The drafts would turn in the river and start back up the long gentle slope to the farm. By the time we arrived back we were more often than not dry as when we started.

I had always wanted to give my own sons a rural upbringing and while they were very small we were able to do that to a certain degree as we lived in a small town and had friends with rural property. So, for awhile, they got to play in wheat fields, and slide down hay chutes, and get bucked off of mean little ponies. To wade in rivers and swim in watering holes. To sleep under star-studded skies and listen to coyotes yip. But life happens as it happens and we had to go where the work was and so ended up in a big city. But I remember a time, when the boys were still small, when I was able to revisit my country life with them and, in so doing, give them a rich rural life memory.

I remember . . . Dust rose behind the pickup as I drove across the hay field, along the grooves that ran deep and permanent across it - originally made by wagon wheels hundreds of years earlier. Scars. Gophers watched from their mounds at the edges of the field, whistling piercing notes of warning before upending themselves into their holes, disappearing from sight with the flick of a black-tipped tail. The truck was a 1965 dust-greyed GMC with standard drive and windows you had to crank manually. One window dropped with a glassy thud a third of the way down; the other stuck on every turn. Once you got it down, you left it down.

The boys and I were helping friends bring in their hay - it was their truck. My sons and I drove slowly along and others hefted the bales into the back of the truck. Each load I drove back to the barn, two stories high, where others lifted the bales into the hayloft. I was driving back over the massive field after my last load. I wore an old denim shirt with sleeves rolled up to the elbows, worn jeans, my hair tied up in a messy, grimy ponytail. Occasionally I spat the dust in my mouth out the window. You can't be a lady when you are haying in the dusty heat of summer. Country was embodied in me - in the way I dressed, the way I moved, the way I didn't think twice about spitting out the truck window while I wrestled with its gears and stubbornness.

My two boys loved riding in that truck. The vast, slippery vinyl seat invited shoving and horse-play. Seatbelts non-existent. The window had a wide ledge and they hung their bellies over it, making themselves dizzy staring at the ground below. When they pulled back into the truck their faces were as dust-grubby as the truck itself. As the day wore on, back and forth, back and forth, they fell asleep in the dozy late-afternoon sun, piled into a corner of the seat like fagged puppies. Their hair stuck out at sweaty angles; there was a burnished redness to their cheeks, an extra freckle or two on their noses. Their lips were parched.

I stopped the truck at the top of a small knoll where there was an ancient medicine wheel, overgrown by hay and grass. As I sat, eyes closed, dust caked in my nostrils and sweat trickling down my back, I listened to the symphony - the country music of birdsong, grasshoppers, red-tailed blackbirds, cows lowing in the distance, and the low purr of a combine on the next farm over. The gentle snores of my sons and the zinging sound of the bluebottle fly battling with the windshield. A day of haying on a Western prairie farm - a day of heat and memory. A son smiling in his sleep.

Here, on Fat Hummingbird Farm, the birdsong may be different. The wind is different and the dust is made up of different rocks and pollen. But the silence is the same. The peace is the same. And here two kids visiting from the city got a wee taste of what their father had had when *he* was little, and what *his* mother and father had when they were small.

"The rooster on that other farm woke me this morning, Nana, and it was singing with the cow!"

OF SUMMER AND PETRICHOR

Tonight I sit on the front porch and, as the moon rises, and the stars blink on, I realize I can smell the season. It flows to my nostrils and elicits smells I had forgotten. Urbanization had dulled our sense of summer smells. This summer, at Fat Hummingbird Farm, is the first complete summertime since we have moved here. We have become aware, again, of the smells of the season in a way I, in particular, have not experienced since we lived on the Prairies. Back in the urban/suburban busyness that we moved from, the prevalent summer smells were that of hot gas fumes as you idled in traffic, or that arid, barren and chemical smell of hot concrete, or the biting odour of a car air conditioner - much like the air on an airplane. There were even a couple of houses on our street whose lawns off-gassed the nose-tweaking fertilizer scent very reminiscent of the white, waxy Weedex bars my father would have us kids drag up and down the lawn when I was a kid. As the season here at the Farm has progressed the scents particular to summer in the country have come as new perfumes or as reminiscences of my partially rural childhood.

Right now everyone seems to be haying. It was a wet spring so getting the crop in was delayed and even dicey. Now tractors rattle up and down our road on a continual basis, hauling trailers loaded to a precarious degree with fat golden rounds of hay. I love the smell of new mown hay. When I am out driving alone I like to roll down the windows and take great gulping inhalations of that wonderful sweet smell. The hay bales, themselves, have a different odour - an underlying sweet but rotting smell that reminds me of the haylofts I played in as a child. Farmers don't pile hay by the barn in huge flaxen mounds anymore. Nothing was more thrilling than taking a running leap out of the mow window and landing in that pile of gold.

Another late summer smell is that of corn silage as it starts to ferment in the silos or under those ubiquitous white tarps peppered with old black tires. Certain kinds of beer still elicit for me the smell of the fermented corn liquor that Grampa Crawford used to make. He hid it in his workshop and swore us kids to secrecy. Gramma Crawford was a deacon for some church or other, he said, and would not approve. But a little corn liquor never hurt *anybody*, he proclaimed.

The summer smell of sweaty horses is a lovely smell - like a fine cheese. But when I have visited horses up and down our road the less lovely smell that is germane only to summer, I think, is the overpowering, eye-watering stench of fly spray. Ooooooh! And then, of course summer is when farm dogs have more frequent interactions with other creatures. Most farm dogs don't really smell that great in the summer because either they have had a run-in with a skunk or have rolled in something unsavoury decomposed to perfection in the summer humidity. Barn wood sweats in the summer too. You can smell the resin and the urine (from dogs usually but sometimes humans too) and that slightly greasy smell of worked wood. You can smell the blood-like smell of rusting nails deep in the seams of the wood.

We have been planting a lot of gardens this summer. I love the smell of the earth when you dig it up to put in perennials. You can inhale that slightly garlic-like smell of earthworms and the scent of the decomposed parts of other plants from years before. The soil is, by turns, wet and dry and loamy and alkaline - and sometimes a dusty acid that you can taste sharply on your tongue. One of the flower beds is under the Black Locust trees. The lovely sweet and dusky smell of the Black Locust trees in bloom - attracting bees, butterflies and hummingbirds alike; dripping its plant-honey onto the back of our shirts, sticking in our hair.

Some plant smells elicit memories. Like the smell of the wild roses. Sweet and pleasing. And the lilacs that bloomed briefly at the beginning of summer. Both the roses and the lilacs remind me of a perfume my mother used to wear - White Shoulders. I was allowed to take a sniff when she held the bottle out to me as she was primping for a night out. But I was never allowed to touch the bottle and, most certainly, could never ask for a dab of the perfume on my own earlobe. White Shoulders was my mother's signature. It drifted after her presence like a shadow when she walked through a room.

Another memory when I walk on the trail and pass the area where our neighbours have their pigs pastured. All summer the pigs have been rooting up the underbrush and turning the soil. The smell of organic materials and exposed roots and insipid darkness evokes the cold, dark essence of the cave my brother and I once found to play in when children - where roots hung from the ceiling and dust dribbled down the walls and there was the sound of a constant wet trickle that we never found the source of.

In winter, washed clothes drape wooden racks situated throughout the house. In summer laundry hangs on the line. And I love the smell of line-dried clothes. I like to bury my face in the clothing that has been scented by sun and by the wind. A little tang of salt sometimes if the wind has been strong over the mountain from the bay. Or sometimes the laundry may have picked up odour from the soil (via the air), especially after a rainfall. Geosmin, which literally translates to 'earth smell', is an organic compound with a distinct earthy flavour and aroma. It's responsible for the earthy taste of beets and contributes to the strong scent that occurs in the air when rains falls after a dry spell of weather - the petrichor (a word derived from that for stone and for the flow in the veins of Greek gods). Regardless of where the scents come from, you simply cannot put that smell into a dryer sheet of a bottle of laundry detergent. The chokecherry bushes are blooming now. If you bruise the twigs or bark they smell distinctly like bitter almonds. The same smell as cyanide I suppose.

Summer is fading now at Fat Hummingbird Farm. I am starting to see a few yellow leaves and the plants in the gardens are starting to get that slightly exhausted look. It has been a particularly dry summer. The kind of parched dry that creates a warm, almost sexual, smell of sweat on ourselves after a day out in the hot sun and dust. When the cellar door opens into the warm air, however, the dank, chilly, musty air drifts out with the distinct odour of field stone walls and cold air - like that icy aroma inside a cave or beside a shadowed brook.

These summer nights have a special smell too. After a hot day where the bedclothes have been baking in the sun through the window, you get into your sheets and they smell like over-ironed shirts - hot and steamy and scorched. Just wait until the moon rises. The moonlight cools them and then they smell like river water

BRIGID & OSTARA*

A roller coaster growing season at Fat Hummingbird Farm. The spring promised to come several times but constantly reneged - sending instead frigid rains and fog-furred days. When she finally did come, she was very late to the ball. Several neighbour farmers by then had gone on to different crops - those that would thrive in a shorter growing season. Pubescent corn fields were tilled up and re-planted with soybeans instead. Deep ruts in the fields caused by heavy machinery out on land still much too wet, stayed the entire summer and have left scars in the soil I am not sure will ever fade. The ruts filled with spring rain waters and brought mosquitoes.

All of our gardens got a late start. After the late, cold spring we had a summer that was so short that, in the month of September, we were still waiting for it to begin. Out in the beds in various parts of the farm, the tomatoes are still green, as are the peppers. The tomatoes should long ago have become vibrant red pasta sauce, and jams, and sun-dried. The potatoes are starchy from inconsistent watering and most of the lettuces bolted. The asparagus looks good for next year, though, and the experiments with cabbage, and broccoli romanesco, and swiss chard have all been very successful. So gardening has been a process this year of learning how to work with a new environment and biosystem. With different timelines and weather oddities. It was expected. At least in part.

Then came hurricane Dorian. And we learned a little more about self-sufficiency and how very important it is that we become that. Our water source is a mountain spring so, unlike a lot of our neighbours on wells, we had water during the lengthy power outages caused by Dorian. But we, unlike a lot of our neighbours, did not have a wood-burning stove. Despite it not being a normally cold time of the year at the time of Dorian, because of the strange weather this year, we were feeling the cold by the time our power came back. Also, in the course of the storm, the roof was ripped from our small, inadequate chicken house. The hens were safely in the garage at the time but it became obvious that that little house would not survive the rigours of an upcoming (and predicted stormy and brutal) winter.

So two things needed to be added to Fat Hummingbird Farm:

1) A new, bigger, better, stronger chicken house. One that would keep the girls safe and secure in inclement weather or safe from marauding predators in the cold and hungry months of winter. Also big enough to store their feed and the feed for the wild birds, two or three bales of straw so that cleaning and replenishing bedding would be easier (and drier!), and room enough for the possible future acquisition of a sheep or two (maybe). We got a local group that provides work and skills training for developmentally, mentally, and emotionally challenged people, to design and build the chicken house. They were so proud of the outcome! 'A thing of beauty', the lead builder remarked. Finished, delivered, and levelled on its footprint beside the garage, it is indeed a thing of beauty. It is substantial - both in size and strength. Next hurricane we, ourselves, could move into it. The girls moved in that very night, having no problem at all with adjustment or transition. They do treat it like a barn, however, laying eggs in little bowls they have made in bales of straw, rather than in the special nesting boxes that were made for them. They treat those with what can only be described as complete disdain as they scratch and toss straw over them. Like a cat does with a meal it doesn't like. The coop is called Ostara.

2) A wood-burning stove. Originally this house had two of them. Both had been removed when the house was renovated. We love the openness of the house renovations along with the plentiful and huge windows. The light was something that drew us both to the house the moment we saw it. But that does mean that it can get chilly. So now a wood-burning stove, red-coloured, named Brigid, graces our living room.

It has pull-out trays that, when next we have a storm-caused power failure, will heat water or soup very nicely. I told you we would end up with a wood-burning stove.

We are still learning the language of wood. Softwood as opposed to hardwood. A face cord as opposed to a full cord. What kind of wood burns best, longest, sweetest, warmest. It is important to learn the different spirits of trees. Here, again, we must look to our self-sufficiency - and to our woods. As we continue to clear parts of our woods to discover the topographical memories hidden under years of wild roses, virginia creeper, and the pasts of the people and creatures and land that pre-dated us, we must also learn the names and spirits of the trees that live here on our land. What trees bear fruit, or nuts, what trees it is best to let stand until their lives are spent, what trees must be sacrificed for the well-being of the others, and what trees must burn - finding their spirits in flame and crackle-sound rather than wind and rain.

And actually a third thing must be added to Fat Hummingbird Farm. The acquisition of an innate knowledge of, and co-existence with, the vagaries, the whims, the inconstancy and inconsistencies of weather, and land, and water, and woods. And acceptance of the fact that those things even apply to our somewhat domesticated gardens. Self-sufficiency is all about acquiring the willingness to bend of the willow and the patience of the owl. And that quality of rolling with the punches . . . but never down for the count.

 * Brigid is the name of the Celtic goddess for fire and Ostara is the name of the Celtic goddess for eggs.

Of Snow & Mad Quilters

Snow has been late coming to Fat Hummingbird Farm this year. There was a skiff here and there during November and December and the faint unfulfilled promise of a white Christmas, but nothing that stayed around. We were told that last year's snow amount was unusual and we didn't find that that was particularly onerous.

But yesterday, in early January, the first blizzard of the season. And more snow in the offing. Meteorologists may perceive snow to be a result of pressure systems and precipitation levels; physicists will recognize the subatomic particles that create snow; but anyone who views the world with a bit of a mystical eye will see snow differently. The mystical eye sees the energy that snow manifests, drawn from the cosmic; and how our minds, our psyche, and soul become illuminated.

The singular charm of viewing snow-draped fields and pastures, trees and outbuildings from each of the windows at Fat Hummingbird Farm is that each is distinctly different.

For instance, out my studio windows, the view is across the farmyard and up the side of the mountain. There the trees are thick in number and varied in species. The snow sits in the branches of each tree dependent on the individual structure of the tree. The snow on the spruce trees lays along the branch, as though they are offering outstretched arms laden with trays of frigid canapés to us. Inviting us to the party. The snow on the oak trees stays snugged in close to the trunk, as though they are holding white-swaddled babies, singing shushing lullabies.

The snow on the tiny tangled twigs of the various kinds of birches makes their appearance even more bouffant. They all look like a gaggle of elderly ladies that are sitting for tea after a day at the hairdressers. All of them with too-tight perms and their hair rinsed the same blue-white. All with the same hairstyle as the hairdresser was only recently graduated from beauty school and knows only one style for 'the mature woman'. The skeletal wild rose and grape vines hold drapes of snow that look for all the world like they are wearing venetian masks - drooping eyeholes and sinister smiles.

Out of our bedroom window, the view is a vast sweep across the valley. When snow-covered it looks like a vast piece of drawing paper. Charcoal hedges and scrub are scrummed in with dull chalk pastels. The bare, stark lines of leafless trees are marked in with the equally stark strokes of a black India ink pen. The snow squalls and drifting snow on the opposite mountain are textured and muted like rubbing charcoal in hard with a sweaty finger - and then erasing it, small bits of pilled paper creating texture. Nearer to the window our pasture denotes its previous life as an orchard, the humped rows delineated and accentuated by the piled snow. The ghosts of old apple trees skitter along the surface with the blowing winds.

Out the living room window that faces the hay field the snow piles around the feet of trees much larger than those in the woods. The snow tries to cling to the limbs and hanging branches of the willows but inevitably slumps to the ground. Depending on the direction of the wind when the snow fell, it will fill the coarse-grained and chapped bark of the beech and maple trees on that one side with snow. You can make out shapes of faces, and countries, and omen and auguries in the patterns of trunk and snow. The snow on the ground in this view is not smooth. It is tangled with the long leftover hay and grasses and thistles.

The view out of the kitchen window is, appropriately so, one of hunger. Here the bird feeders hang. Birds suspend from them, fly to and from them, hover around them - like a swarm of bees with no place to go. The starlings drop to the rain barrels below for the fallen seeds, brooming the snow from the top of the barrels with their wings, making them look like an ugly/pretty version of a street sweeper. The snow in this view looks like a quilt - the tracks of many different kinds of birds stitching back and forth and around and around like the stitching has been done by a mad, crazed quilter with crossed eyes.

There is rain predicted - and that will change the views. And snow again, and change again. The windows will reveal new shapes, new forms, new snow. That is, if you don't think like a meteorologist or a physicist, but like a mystic.

She Will Tell Me Where the Deer Sleep

The winter is starting to lose its grip on our land, on our small farm on the side of the mountain. The days still threaten snow and realize that snow in the night. But there are days of rain, too. Icy, chilling rain but also rain that falls fat and soft and turns the pillowed snow to the consistency of melting ice cream. And now are the songs of birds that have been gone too long from this place – coming back on the warming breezes. Now is the time to leave the somnolence of the wood-burning stove. To pull on boots against the mud and a coat, still, against the wind and venture out to see our land. And to truly see what the land is revealing to us after its winter slumber, I must learn to be open again.

Place needs a witness. As I ramble the still-sodden hayfield, the woods still bare-limbed but song-filled, the stream running free again – loosed from its frozen bed, I bear witness to the stories, the form, and the spirit of our little farm. I cannot view this place indifferently, distantly, or without empathy. I cannot just *look*, I cannot use only my eyes. I must actually behold– spiritually. I must also hearken, not just hear. As I have intent, sense, and heart – so does nature, so does this place.

To truly observe the spirit of my farm, I must leave my camera in the kitchen; my notebook beside it. I must sometimes set both words and the creation of image aside. To inhabit place is to do so much more deeply than either image or words can allow. It is like when sitting motionless on a stump in the forest, a butterfly lands on my knee. If I try and grab my camera, no matter if inch by inch, it will fly away. If I say something, or even gasp, the mere current of my breath will lift its wings and it will leave. I can only go under, submerge to where I just experience the butterfly. I note the tear in her wing, the way she bathes her face with wire-thin legs; the way her tongue rolls and unrolls like a party favour. When she eventually flies away, I hope only that she remembers that I was kind.

I am in great need of a dog, a dog like I used to have, that taught me about place. We have acquired a new puppy – a large mixed-breed pup that we hope will become a great, old farm dog. The kind that follows us from chore to chore, sleeps on the porch in the heat of the day, and thinks it makes perfect sense to go out with you late at night just to look at the moon. Maybe even howl at it together. Right now she is gangly – loose skinned, floppy-limbed, all tail and ears and feet she has yet to grow into. No sense of her own or others' personal space; with a lovely and loving naivety that everyone must, of course, love her. Big, clumsy feet that bring a lot of the outside . . . inside.

This pup, she must grow to *know* our farm, this place. The pup charges at this land like she must eat it up. Her enthusiasm explodes birds from the brush and splashes mud on the chickens. She doesn't know yet how to share what she experiences with *me*. The old dog I had before her, a slow and deliberate Lab, taught me to see, to know where I am. She of advancing age and myself of aching bones meant we muddled along languidly. Our pace was slow, convoluted, measured . . . astonished.

A dog knows the passage of time – more keenly, and *differently* than do we. They can tell from the strength of a scent whether an animal came by here hours ago, or days ago. They know the weave, and the tuning, and the turning of seasons; when to expect geese nesting in the grasses and when the turtles will rise to the surface after a winter sheathed in frigid mud.

Conversely, walking into place with a dog *stops* all time. She takes time to savour. The scents pull her like the fingered aromas from a bakery shop. She finds berries dropped by birds and perceives whether they were dropped by a crow or a chickadee. She knows where the skunk slept last night; she can follow the skip and leap of a hunting coyote. She alerts me to the swaying tails of salmon under the sheen of the water in spawning season – mesmerizing, spellbinding. She knows the branch on the ground is newly fallen.

Being in place with a dog means that walking is determined by circumstance, not the route or the pace. Circumstances create irregularity, doubling back, stopping so suddenly one gasps. Counselled by the dog, I notice that there is a new pile of leaves, and that the air has moistened with a lifting fog. It means that sometimes I have to get down to ground level to see the infant geese hidden at the riverside; that sometimes I have to look up to see the heron bizarrely in the tree; that sometimes I should turn and see what made that small, barely-there sound. When her ears go up, I should look to what is rustling in the bush. As she sniffs intently at a circular, swirled indentation in the long grasses, I realize the sleeping places of deer in the night. If we feel that we are the 'other' in place, it can close us. A dog, in her exuberant 'rolling' in the world, in her generous sharing of her understanding of place, shows us how to open.

The pup will learn to witness our land. She will learn to share the rhythms with me. Next year, when winter again recedes, she will walk the farm with me. She will show me where the deer sleep.

Of Choirs & Choruses & Silence

Does sound have rhythm? Does it rise and fall like the massive tides on the Bay of Fundy? Does it come and go? Does it have the levels of tone like the wind? Does it have conversations? Does it vibrate? Does it hum in E flat?

The first greening of the grasses and the small budding leaves on various trees all over our land and up the mountain are a blessed sight to the eyes. But, equally, they have sounds - muted, subdued, perhaps only suggested. But they are there. Listen. Listen closely enough and you can hear the sweet 'pop' of a bud unfurling its wee leaves; and a shushing pulsing sound as the trees and plants push the green up through their stems and trunks and out into the very tips of themselves. Like a steady and assured heartbeat. I swear the crocuses each bloom with the faint tinkle of a fairy bell. The apple trees are coming into bloom and with that a small, reedy cheer of 'ta-da' erupts with each flower. Each dandelion blows open its bloom with a cheery 'ka-pow!'. Dandelions are not dainty or exquisite but instead their unvarnished beauty and vigour creates an unbridled enthusiasm. A field of them is suggestive of a filled arena at a sports event. All that fervent cheering. The lilac blossoms literally creak as they slowly open petal by petal - the sound staying true to prairie rocking chairs and the scraping sound of hawks' wings in the wind.

Now is the sound of laundry snapping on the line - the wind a rushing cataract sound lifting the shirt sleeves and pant legs and billowing the sheets like an incoming wave on the Bay of Fundy. The intimate garments titter and giggle as the breezes caress them. Their pastel colours seem more blushed as a result of being out on the line. The clack/plonk sound of unclipping clothes pegs and dropping them into the wicker basket as each dried, sun-warmed and scented piece of laundry is removed.

And, of course, here on the farm where the birds are plentiful and diverse, birdsong is rampant. They are a combined choir and symphony of avian melodies and harmonies. They start early, even before dawn, and continue until the morning wanes to midday. Their calls - the twittering and chattering and cheeping and cooing and cawing and whistles and screeches, the rolling up of notes, the rolling down of notes, the chortling, the murmuring - interweave with the sunlight and follow the shadows. At midday, things quiet for awhile. Then, the dove coos are audible and gentle, the knock-knock of the woodpecker discernible, the whining buzz of the hummingbirds resounding. Then the chickens under the hedges can be heard to be muttering along in counterpoint. The turkey buzzards high in the sky, circling, circling do not have a call. But you can imagine the soft thup. thup sound of their alternating ascending and descending coils. If you listen closely enough. Like riding in a silent glider high above the fields.

If birds are the orchestra of the morning then peepers are the choir of the evening. The evening is cooling, darkness slowly descends. Then . . . . that unearthly ambiance, that froggy melody. It is like the night has a pulse. It is the sound that creates the pleasant background music for a glass of wine on the evening porch - along with the incinerating sound of immolating moths around the porch light or the clicking on and off sound of the fireflies in the pasture.

Late at night the foxes, and coyotes, and owls, and coy-wolves take the stage. The foxes and owls screech like they are playing the role of a murdered woman. The scream of British mystery series and disturbing movies. The sounds you hear and wonder if it is human after all, but have no intention of investigating. The coyotes and coy-wolves start their music when the moon is high - running the fields and coursing the riverbed.

When sound has become so true. So honest. So pure here on Fat Hummingbird Farm . . . well, even the moon has a sound. The finger-nail sliver of a crescent moon has a sharp, clear snip sound. It keens in a G7. Above the harmonies of the peepers and slow rocky babble of the stream, it sings. But the full moon sings best. Above the branches of the tallest trees - the trees that night-whisper in the midnight breeze - spreading her wide, wide skirts and looking down with a bemused smile in her pitted face she begins - a bone-thrumming hum in low E. Listen.

A Requiem and Canticle for Place

We have been here for two years. Being here has taught me that the freshness, the crispness, the originality, the rawness of the country is tied to the blood that surges through my heart. I have been taught that that blood is tied to the flowing rhythms of earth and rivers; sky and clouds; weather and seasons. This lesson is utmost.

But I have also learned a few other lessons, a few 'home truths' as my mother used to call them.

1. The value of silence and open space

I am not saying the silence is complete. There are chickens bickering and dogs barking and the sound of the chainsaw in our neighbour's woods. There is the rattle and bang as logging trucks hit the pothole in the road near our house. But I mean the overall peace of things. How the chirrr of the cicadas on a warm afternoon lull me into a doze. How the trilling of the peepers in the dark of night act like a soporific lullaby. There is space, land, at Fat Hummingbird Farm. And in that space I can stretch my arms, I can stretch my legs, I can stretch my sight and my mind. And within that space is peace. And, truth be told, if you ignore the occasional sour note, the bickering chickens do actually sing. Quietly, in a sedate muttered timbre. An undertone to the songbirds' constant joyful hymns.

2. The importance of earthworms

Earthworms are valuable to one's soil and are like the miner's canary - lack of them denotes poor soil and land that is in need. As a child, after a rainstorm, I could often be found on the front sidewalk, in tears, vainly attempting to resuscitate drowned earthworms by picking them up and throwing them back into the dirt. Now I am aware of how very important they are to the soil, to our land. I still pick them up and throw them back to the dirt when I find them - racing the chickens so the worms have a chance to burrow back into the soil before they become chicken cuisine. I have learned to squeeze soil in my hand to see how arable it is. If an earthworm crawls between your fingers in the process this is a good thing. I feel, unlike when I was a child, that I am finally saving them - encouraging them to stay and live on our land. Turning our land from needful to thankful.

3. Everything relies on the weather

Weather is one of the greatest unknowns. The seasons are fairly consistent, overall. We will eventually move from one to the other. Intellectually we know this. But the first spring was long, cold, and very wet. We (and the farmers around us) were about a month behind in growing. The water from mountain springs dribbled a good lengthy soak down our hayfield making it still, in June, boggy and wet. We had taken to calling it a 'water meadow', as I knew them in England. A field that floods with water when there is a lot of rain - in our case exacerbated by the springs streaming down from the mountains. We check the weather first thing when we get up and the next day's weather last thing at night. It is about the only section of the evening news-hour on TV that we actually watch. Not convinced that either the weather person or our phone weather app is telling the complete truth, we obsessively keep checking for changes throughout the day. We decide on farm chores to be completed on any given day by the 'percentage' of rain certainty or how strong the wind will be blowing. The weather decides for us on what days colourful rows of laundry will hang in yards up and down the roads. The weather dictates how many tractors rumble up and down on the road in front of the house with seeder, or harrower, or thresher in tow. Whether they rumble hurriedly or leisurely.

4. There is joy in small things

Back in the city, sightings of new blooms or such things were, for the most part, inconsequential or unimportant. But I have found that since we have come to Fat Hummingbird Farm, those same things have become momentous. I have been watching the ditches and hills for lupines. They were blooming at the time that we arrived and I was so taken with them. I am looking for them now as a sort of 'anniversary' event. The first tree swallow to come and nest in a neighbour's bird box is noteworthy, as are the arrival of barn swallows to the new barn across the road. The first wood turtle to emerge from the frozen mud is eagerly anticipated. We await tornadoes of chimney swifts and the swoop of bats emerging from winter hibernations. The Black Locusts have been taking their sweet time leafing out and I watch every day to see if their honeyed flowers have yet bloomed. The wild phlox can be depended on, though, and lines our stream bed and ditches with their white and purple blooms. And, of course, the wee creature for which our farm was named - the hummingbirds - were knocking at our windows right on time in May, impolitely demanding that their feeders be put out. So far we appear to have a half dozen of them. Babies abound - calves, lambs, piglets, rabbits, birds, squirrels, racoons, foxes, foals, and fawns. Each sighting of a new baby in a field or pasture or tree is a celebratory moment.

5. Having a farm is a hell of a lot of work

We knew we would be 'starting over', that there would be a lot of work involved in building the gardens like the ones we had left behind. We knew also, at least hypothetically, that we would have more and different challenges to growing things than we had had in suburbia. We have far more stone than we knew. The soil is far more clay than arable. The farm has not been worked in any way for a very, very long time. Where the plants and fruit trees and flowers may be slow to adjust and grow, the weeds are not. Where we fight the water where it should not be in some places we must come up with inventive ideas to get the water to other places where it needs to be. The front door screen no longer fits the frame after two winters of cold and has basically disintegrated and some shingles have disappeared from the side of the house in the winter winds. We have had racoons in the ceiling and squirrels in the walls. We were unable to live trap any of them. Removing all of the deadfall that the spring thaw reveals is a BIG job.

But we have also had so much help. A neighbour helps to keep our hayfield in check by taking the hay off occasionally. He helps to keep our pasture in check by putting his cows and calves on it periodically. Another neighbour shared the cost of a tractor mower so we can have some control over the grass on the couple of acres the house sits on and up around the berry bushes - making tick hunting a little easier for the hens. Yet another neighbour has offered his digger to dig a trench to control the water in the water meadow. Another neighbour has offered their teenaged kids to help with some of the grunt work. Another neighbour plows out our driveway and mailbox in the winter. And yet another brought a truckload of manure for our gardens and, when bringing it, brought along his own work crew of his two sons so all the work of shovelling it into the field did not fall to us.

6. The country road is community

When we first moved here we would walk our country road. We knew next to no one along it; we were strangers who sometimes received a tentative wave from a porch, or were ignored. Now we have a goodly sense of who is in what house, what the history of that house and sometimes the family is. We know a lot of people by name - can lift a hand in a heart-felt wave and have it returned just as heartily. Sometimes we get invited in for tea or, conversely, do the inviting in for coffee. Our porch has become a communication portal. Friends honk when they drive by. And we honk when we drive by their places up and down the road. People call out hellos on their walks, or jogs, or cycles past the house. We can watch the daily habits and chores of other farmers from the front porch. The postman enjoys it when he has an excuse (a parcel!) to come up our driveway; he admires our heritage chickens and always has a word or two about the weather and how often it makes him cut his grass. When we are walking on our country road he waves as he passes us - as does the UPS man. Once a neighbour and friend rode her horses up our driveway just to say hello. When she canters along the track below our pasture she whoops and waves. When we walk the country road now it is a means of communication, of community. We belong.

7. A farm is alive

Fat Hummingbird Farm was part of a land grant that originated in 1784 and has been actively farmed in one way or another since 1872. We live on a farm that was part forest, part wetlands, part orchard, and part pasture. All those parts tell something of our farm's past. We live with animals both domesticated and wild, with plants, with flowers, with a garden. I walk on this land every day and never get bored. Over the course of these two years I have seen that there is always something new to see and learn. I sit on my porch, which oversees our pasture, another pasture, and beyond that the river and the valley and watch the cows graze, or the turkey buzzards circling high up in the sky, or the wisps of burning brush on the opposite mountain. Hummingbirds buzz me as they careen from feeder to feeder and there is the constant comings and goings of heavy bumblebees.

The soul-quenching realization that the farm is very much alive - the non-human around us, the flora and fauna, are profoundly aware and responsive. The Black Locust trees talk constantly. They are a favourite roost of the hummingbirds that seem to delight in their conversations. Cows play with each other, they form friendships, and calves even become best friends - seeking each other out first thing in the morning when their mothers send them out to play. Chickens panic loudly if they have misplaced the rest of their flock, calling and calling until they are back together again - a community. Willows can physically move themselves close to water. Seeds can hold themselves back from germinating and then erupt like fireworks when you walk past them. The wind can bring the smell of seashells and salt down the mountain to blend with the heady smell of timothy hay. Birds sing the sun up and peepers sing the moon up. We can't do that.

So . . . just a few of the things I have learned in our time here. I guess, basically, Place, this farm, needs a witness. I cannot view this place indifferently, distantly, nor without empathy. I cannot just look, I cannot use only my eyes. I must actually behold this farm - spiritually. I must also hearken - not just hear. As we, ourselves, have intent, sense, heart - so does this place, this farm. David Abram, the philosopher and naturalist, said that each place has its own mind, its own psyche - a place-specific intelligence shared by we humans that dwell in this place of Fat Hummingbird Farm. But it is also shared by the coyotes yapping in the valley, by the foxes and the spiders, the ferns and the wild phlox. By all of us beings that live at Fat Hummingbird Farm. We are staying. Knowledge of this place and where we are is intertwined with the knowledge of who we are. We are home.